RECIPES AND REFLECTIONS FROM

CALIFORNIA'S HEARTLAND

RECIPES AND REFLECTIONS FROM

CALIFORNIA'S HEARTLAND

VOLUME I

COMMEMORATING THE AGRICULTURE AND CUISINE OF CALIFORNIA

By the producers of the television series California Heartland

KVIE CHANNEL 6 • SACRAMENTO

PHOTOGRAPHY BY INVISION PICTURES • SACRAMENTO

Published by KVIE Channel 6
2595 Capitol Oaks Drive
PO Box 6
Sacramento, California 95812
www.californiaheartland.org

FIRST EDITION

All excerpts, recipes and photography used by permission.

Executive Editor: Jan Tilmon, KVIE Channel 6, Sacramento, California
Editor: Jim O'Donnell, KVIE Channel 6, Sacramento, California
Assistant Editor: Christine Watson, KVIE Channel 6, Sacramento, California
Writer: Jerry Blair, KVIE Channel 6, Sacramento, California
Recipe Editors: Rich Seiber, Caroline Adams, KVIE Channel 6, Sacramento, California
Art Direction and Design: Michelle Branton, Branton Image Design, Suisun City, California
Food Stylist: Tom Thompson, InVision Pictures, Sacramento, California
Food Photography: Tom Thompson, InVision Pictures, Sacramento, California
Heartland Photographer: Martin Christian, KVIE Channel 6, Sacramento, California
Print Manager: Joe Zaniker, Graphic Focus, Sacramento, California

Library of Congress Cataloging-in-Publication Data is available upon request.

ISBN 9674099-2-6

FOREWORD

California Heartland is a weekly public television series that celebrates the generous earth of the Golden State...its beauty, bounty, and the people who bring food and comfort to our nation and the world.

We couldn't have imagined when we began this journey five years ago that a television show about agriculture would have such universal appeal. Unique in its style and its subject, the show has captured the imagination of Californians both young and old—from Los Angeles urbanites to Central Valley heartland dwellers. Nearly a million viewers tune in each and every week. The talented television professionals that produce the series have traveled throughout California to farms, fairs, festivals, ranches and rodeos, to tell more than 600 stories from the heartland. They have become fans of the dedicated, innovative people who grow, nurture and provide agriculture's bounty.

Charismatic *Heartland* host George Reading, with his velvet voice and touch, has embraced his role as spokesperson. "It is really about us, all of us," he says, "our roots are in the earth...our culture...and our history."

And of course, it's about the wonderful food. In the vast expanse of California, we have people from all cultures that delight in preparing dishes from the state's agricultural bounty. The enthusiastic and loyal viewers of *California Heartland* inspired us to create this book. The Web site, www.californiaheartland.org, simply sizzles with requests every time the show features a California 'fresh' recipe. So we gathered the best. This is one of those great cookbooks that bring together recipe favorites from many contributors. You'll find recipes from famous restaurant chefs we have featured on the show, and our favorites from food festivals throughout the heartland. There are recipes from viewers who have generously shared family dishes handed down through generations. And some very special recipes come from the *Heartland* crew—they are great 'cooks' in their own right. A sweet contribution comes from *California Heartland's* Allison Thompson—"Lemon Love Notes"—the recipe and her memories are a loving gift from her Grandmother.

As your favorite recipes bake or simmer, we hope you will enjoy browsing through the book. We couldn't resist also sharing Reflections from the Heartland that depict some of what we have learned and experienced on our journey.

—Jan Tilmon
Executive Editor
KVIE Channel 6

RECIPES FROM THE HEARTLAND

APPETIZER

SOUP & SALAD

ENTREE

SIDE DISH

DESSERT

SAUCES, DIPS & DRESSINGS

BEVERAGE

"LET'S DO A BOOK!"

It was like saying "let's put on a play in the backyard—we need costumes, a set...and stars!" Instead we said "let's do a cookbook and publish it ourselves—we need fabulous recipes, a writer, a designer, a food stylist/chef/photographer...and stars!" No Problem! Rich Seiber and Caroline Adams went to work selecting viewer favorites from the TV show—and the California Heartland team contributed their own delicious delights. Food preparation, presentation and photography demanded the very best. Fortunately, our dear friend Tom Thompson counts among his potpourri of professional credits these very skills. For weeks Tom shopped, chopped, tasted and tested—and when perfected, he photographed the sumptuous recipes in this book.

We wanted even more. We wanted to share what we have discovered in the heartland through words and photographs. So we turned to Jerry Blair, writer, poet... and *California Heartland's* Executive Producer for Specials. Jerry contributed his own "reflections" and selected the words of other great heartland observers—such as Dr. Kevin Starr, California State Librarian and its leading historian. Then we asked California Heartland's Emmy winning videographer, Martin Christian, to contribute his still photographs...reflections of times past and present. There was never a question about who would lead us through design and printing. Michelle Branton of Branton Image Design had guided us with a steady and creative hand through our foray into publishing our annual *California Heartland Fairs and Festivals Calendar*, along with Joe Zaniker of Graphic Focus. With patience, professionalism and good humor, Michelle designed this new creation. With so many cooks in the kitchen...we needed a Project Manager—who became Editor by the end of this adventure... and of course it had to be Jim O'Donnell, KVIE's Director of Communications. As we insiders know—Jim needs a little 'managing' himself and he turned to organized and meticulous cookbook connoisseur Christine Watson for an able assist.

And Stars? Never any shortage of those. There is of course, the heartland and its rich bounty that begets the fabulous food, inspires the words, and presents the natural beauty to be photographed. And there are the *California Heartland* STARS...Corita Gravitt—*California Heartland's* Executive Producer/Writer, superstar host George Reading, Senior Producer/Reporter Pat McConahay, Reporter/Producer Allison Thompson, Registered Dietitian Michele Lites, Videographer/ Photographers Martin Christian and Aimee McKinney, Coordinating Producer Rich Seiber, Unit Manager Scott Moniak, Production Assistants Katrina Heim-Tupper, Sorrell Fowler, Staff Assistant Caroline Adams, Editors Karen Eckert and James Mastrandrea, Graphics Designer Jamie Judd and Post Production Supervisor Jim Calahan, and Bob Vice—our constant and greatest ally. And least we forget the "original"—Van Gordon Sauter, who in his wisdom said "California ought to have a farm show"...well Van, we have a farm show, a calendar, and now a book...all celebrating the generous earth of the Golden State.

How fortunate we are to have them all. We are able to share the bounty with you because of the generous support of the sponsors who have made *California Heartland* possible...The California Farm Bureau Federation; Cal Farm and Allied Insurance-members of Nationwide Insurance; The California Milk Advisory Board, The California Almond Board, The California Department of Food and Agriculture, The California Integrated Waste Management Board, Dow AgriSciences, The California Beef Council, The California Agriculture Network, and Monsanto Foundation.

FEEDING THE WORLD

Over one hundred and fifty years ago the pioneers moving west had a dream of California as garden of the world. Today that dream has been fulfilled.

The initial perception of California on the part of the Spaniards and Latinos who settled here in the late 18th century was not that this was some busy, fertile never-never land. They had a sense of what it is; semi-arid and arid in many cases, requiring irrigation. The Latino settlers in California did not invest in a major way in agriculture. Their export product was in their cattle.

Initially it was hard enough to get products within California where they were needed. For instance, to get the dairy products, the fresh fruits and produce in the Bay Area into Sacramento and up to the mining areas. The great garden of California had to be invented.

Beginning with the export of wheat, in the 1870s and accelerating into the 1880s and '90s, California was announcing to the rest of the world that it had the capacity to be a vast and continuous garden.

—Dr. Kevin Starr, State Librarian

CHOCOLATE SHEET CAKE

SERVES 8
Submitted by Tom Thompson - cookbook photographer

2 - cups granulated sugar
2 - cups all-purpose flour
1 - teaspoon cinnamon
1 - stick of margarine (1/4 lb)
1/2 - cup cocoa, bitter and unsweetened
1/2 - cup white Crisco
1 - cup water
2 - eggs, slightly beaten
1 - teaspoon vanilla extract
1 - cup buttermilk
1 - teaspoon baking soda (dissolved in buttermilk first)

FROSTING:
1 - stick of butter (1/4 lb)
1/3 - cup milk
1/4 - cup cocoa, unsweetened
1 - box (1 lb) powdered sugar
1 - teaspoon vanilla extract
1 - cup chopped pecans, lightly toasted

FOR SPECIAL PRESENTATION:
1 - cup powdered sugar
heavy cream, enough to make sugar slightly liquid

1 Place first three ingredients (sugar, flour and cinnamon) in a large bowl. Combine margarine, cocoa, Crisco and water in sauce pan and bring to a boil. Remove from heat and pour over the dry ingredients (set aside earlier in a large bowl.) Add the eggs, vanilla extract, buttermilk and baking soda. Mix well.

2 Grease a cookie sheet (at least 10" x 15" x 1" in size.) The depth is important to prevent spill over. Pour batter into the cookie sheet and place in a preheated 400 degree oven on the center rack. Bake exactly 20 minutes. To check for doneness, press cake lightly to see if it springs back.

FROSTING:

3 Place butter, milk and cocoa in a saucepan and bring to a boil. Remove from heat and add powdered sugar, vanilla extract and pecans. Mix well. Pour hot over warm cake. Cut cake into 3" squares and serve with a scoop of vanilla ice cream on the side.

FOR SPECIAL PRESENTATION:

4 Cut out circles of the cake with a large biscuit cutter (3" across.) Prepare the Chocolate Port Sauce (see recipe on page 35) and pour a puddle of sauce onto each serving plate—enough to fill the bottom of the plate.

5 Mix powdered sugar with heavy cream until sugar is slightly liquid and place in a small pastry bag with a small round tip. Pipe the sugar into the chocolate puddle in a spiral design starting at the center. Drag the point of a sharp knife through the chocolate and sugar in a zig-zag pattern. Place the cake in the center of the chocoalte sauce and top with 3 raspberries and a small sprig of mint. ✣

This recipe has been in the family for more than 60 years and is our all-time favorite. It is a cross between cake and brownies. Very easy to make!

HEARTLAND DIET

"When you look at the American diet in the 19th Century there was meat and potatoes, a lot of salted and pickled foods. Oranges would be a luxury. Then because of California, the American diet broadened out to include oranges almost all year long, lemons, fresh fruit and vegetables. It democratised what previously had been a rather elite menu."

—Dr. Kevin Starr, State Librarian

California has 83,000 farms generating $58 billion in personal income for Californians. The state has led the nation in total farm production every year since 1948. The heartland is the nation's salad bowl, harvesting more than half of the nation's fresh vegetables.

RUSTIC APRICOT CHERRY GALETTE

SERVES 4–6
Submitted by Beverly Berkley of David Berkley's Fine Wines & Specialty Foods

PASTRY:
1 1/4 - cups all-purpose flour
2 - Tablespoons granulated sugar
1/2 - cup plus 1 Tablespoon unsalted butter, chilled and diced
pinch of salt
3 - Tablespoons ice cold water

FILLING:
2 lbs - ripe apricots
20 - large ripe Bing cherries, pitted (about 1 cup)
2 - Tablespoons flour
3/4 - cup granulated sugar

PASTRY:

1 In a mixer or food processor, combine flour, sugar and salt. Add butter and mix. Then add enough water to make dough come together. Allow dough to rest in refrigerator for at least 2 hours.

FILLING:

2 Wash apricots, cut in half, remove pit and slice. Wash cherries, pit, cut in half. Toss fruit with flour and sugar. Set aside.

3 Roll out pastry to 1/4" thick and into a 14" circle. Place in a pie pan or 12" tart pan. Fill the center with 1/3 of the fruit mixture. Fold up pastry edges over fruit leaving the center open. The amount of fruit will make three of these tarts. Refrigerate at least 30 minutes. Preheat the oven to 400 degrees.

4 Brush chilled dough with egg whites and sprinkle with granulated sugar. Bake for approximately 1 hour. If pastry is getting too dark, after 40 minutes, cover with foil to prevent burning. Serve with a giant dollop of whipped cream or a scoop of vanilla low fat frozen yogurt. ✣

GRILLED ASPARAGUS WITH MARINATED SHIITAKE

SERVES 4–6
Submitted by Chef Yoshi Kojima - of mc²

20 - large pieces of asparagus
8 - Shiitake mushrooms
1 - teaspoon capers
1 - Roma tomato, diced
2 - Tablespoons shallots, chopped
1/2 - Tablespoon fresh parsley, chopped
4 - fresh basil leaves, julienned
3/4 - cup extra virgin olive oil
2 - Tablespoons balsamic vinegar
lemon juice to taste

1 Mix capers, diced tomato, shallots, parsley, basil, oil, lemon juice and balsamic vinegar in a bowl to create marinade. Heat olive oil in a saute pan and cook mushrooms on a very high heat. Add the marinade. Rub the asparagus with olive oil and grill until it is tender and cooked all the way through.

2 Serve asparagus and shiitakes with marinade drizzled on top. ✣

MUIR'S CENTRAL VALLEY

"The time will undoubtedly come when the entire area of this noble valley will be tilled like a garden, when the fertilizing waters of the mountains, now flowing to the sea, will be distributed to every acre...."
—John Muir

It was in the late 1800s that environmentalist and sometime farmer John Muir predicted the fertile future in store for California's heartland. Muir saw the agricultural potential in the rich soil of the Sacramento and San Joaquin Valleys and recognized the untapped promise of Sierra Nevada water. The irrigation projects developed by the state and the Bureau of Reclamation were foreseen by Muir as a grand plan of agricultural production and land conservation. Because of Muir's foresight and standards of conservation, California has become a worldwide leader in the production of agricultural products and is leading the fight to preserve the heartland's grandeur and beauty.

AWARD WINNING AGRICULTURE

Since the beginning of organized agriculture, celebration of the harvest has been a ritual practiced by those who produce from the land. In California's early days, farmers and ranchers would travel across the heartland with families in tow and gather at fairgrounds to reflect on their success and share "the cream of the crop." They'd relax, be entertained, but mostly, they'd compete for a coveted blue ribbon, proof that their product was the best in the region. That award represented a level of quality that all farmers would strive for…that your prize bull would be the breeding standard for the area, and the honored crops would provide the seed your fellow farmers would buy and sow. As for the best peach pie…well, besides bragging rights for the next year, it was just good eating!

BABA GHANOUSH (EGYPTIAN APPETIZER)

SERVES 8–10

Submitted by Corita Gravitt - California Heartland Executive Producer

2 lbs - eggplant, peeled, cooked and crushed
2 - cloves garlic, minced (or more to taste)
2 - Tablespoons lemon juice
3/4 - cup tomatoes, chopped
1 - Tablespoon olive oil
salt and pepper to taste
2 - Tablespoons mint, chopped

1 Combine all ingredients, reserving a bit of mint to sprinkle on top of the dip. Serve with warm wedges of pita bread. Sprinkle paprika lightly on top of dip for additional color. ✣

BBQ FAJITAS ON A SKEWER

SERVES 4

Submitted by Beverly Berkley of David Berkley's Fine Wines & Specialty Foods

1/2 lb - boneless beef top sirloin, cut 1" thick
1 - each green, yellow and red bell peppers
2 - sweet onions, 1 red, 1 white
(like Walla Walla or Maui)
8 - low fat fajita size tortillas
Salsa Fresca (see recipe below)

MARINADE:
2 - fresh limes, juiced
1 - Tablespoon corn oil
1 - teaspoon ground cumin seeds
1 - teaspoon chili powder
1 - Tablespoon fresh garlic, finely chopped

1 Soak 16 (9") bamboo skewers in water for 10 to 15 minutes, then drain just before you are ready to assemble and barbecue. Trim all fat from the steak. Cut the beef crosswise into 1/2" strips. Thread the strips onto 8 of the skewers, weaving them back and forth. Cut the peppers and onions into square chunks and thread them onto the remaining 8 skewers, alternating colors for eye appeal.

2 In a small bowl, combine marinade ingredients of lime juice, oil, garlic and spices. Mix well, then brush onto each of the skewers.

3 Cook the vegetables first over the hot part of the grill for approximately 10 to 13 minutes, then move them to the outside, cooler edge of the grill.

4 Place the beef skewers over the hot part of the grill. Cook for 8 to 10 minutes over medium heat— turning once.

5 Just before the beef is done, place several tortillas at a time on the grill to warm them. Wrap tortillas in paper towels in a basket. Serve fajitas with salsa fresca. ✣

SALSA FRESCA

Submitted by Beverly Berkley of David Berkley's Fine Wines & Specialty Foods

2 - cups ripe tomatoes, diced
2 - fresh jalapeño peppers, finely chopped
1/2 - medium red onion, finely chopped
2 - fresh limes, juiced
3/4 - teaspoon salt
2 - Tablespoons fresh cilantro, chopped
1 - Tablespoon olive oil

1 Blend all items together. Allow flavors to meld before serving with BBQ Fajitas or as a chip dip. Keep chilled. ✣

AG & THE WEATHER

"Everybody talks about the weather but nobody does anything about it."
—Robert Johnson

Farmers are held hostage by the weather. Plagued by "el Nino" and his cantankerous sibling "la Nina," heartland growers often don't know whether they're coming or going when it comes to the weather.

Try as it might to lessen the blow of inclement weather, the weather service, with all its technological expertise can do little more than give hope and solace to the wary farmer.

With crops in the fields and harvests looming, the weather worries that badger the people who work the soil are an integral part of being a farmer in California's heartland.

BLUEBERRY PIE

SERVES 6–8
Submitted by Green Valley Farm - Sonoma County

1 - 10" baked pie shell
6 - cups blueberries
(a one pint dry basket = 3 cups)
1/2 - cube (1/4 cup) butter
4 1/2 - Tablespoons lemon juice
3 - Tablespoons flour
1/3 - teaspoon salt
3/4 - cup granulated sugar
3/4 - cup brown sugar
1/4 - teaspoon almond extract*

1 Mix together the flour, salt, sugar, brown sugar and almond extract, then add them to a mixture of 3 cups of blueberries, butter, and lemon juice. Cook over medium heat until the mixture thickens. If necessary, you may add a little more flour or corn starch to the mixture to make it thicken more quickly. Remove from heat and let cool.

2 Add 3 cups raw blueberries. Mix gently and pour into baked pie shell. Serve plain or with whipped cream or ice cream. You can take a short cut with the pie crust by using the refrigerated pre-made pie crust, placed in your own baking dish. ✣

*SECRET INGREDIENT = almond extract

BOYSENBERRY PIZZA

SERVES 6–8
Submitted by Vella Farms - Modesto

4 - cups boysenberries
1 1/2 - cups granulated sugar
1 - cube (1/2 cup) butter, softened
1 - cup flour
1/4 - cup powdered sugar
8 oz - cream cheese, softened
2 - tablespoons cornstarch

1 Stir and mix boysenberries and 1 cup of sugar. Set aside to draw juice while you prepare the balance of recipe.

CRUST:
2 Mix together butter, flour and powdered sugar to form a soft ball. Spread with fingers in a 12" round pizza pan. Crust will be thin. Bake for 15 minutes at 325 degrees. Check at 12 minutes to see if crust is lightly golden brown. When crust is done, set it aside to cool.

CREAM CHEESE LAYER:
3 Cream together cream cheese and 1/2 cup sugar. Spread over crust after it is cooled slightly (10 minutes).

TOPPING:
4 Pour berries into a large strainer, catching juice. Measure juice and add water, if necessary to make 1 3/4 cups liquid. Gradually add liquid to 2 Tablespoons of cornstarch. Cook over medium heat stirring constantly until mixture thickens. Boil 1 minute longer. Add berries to glaze mixture, stirring gently to cover all berries. Pour over top of cream cheese layer. Chill at least 2 to 3 hours before serving. Must be refrigerated to keep it from running. ✣

This is an excellent recipe that can be prepared off season by using frozen blackberries.

SOLANO'S GOLD

It has been called "Solano's Gold." It is just as valuable as the treasured ore, but in Solano county the "gold" is the rich tradition of orchard farming.

In the 1800s most of the attention went to the Mother Lode of the Sierra. But a few daring souls found their way to Solano county where their efforts went toward establishing a thriving agricultural community.

Almonds, cherries, peaches, pears, plums...the list is long. Thousands of acres of thriving orchards established the county as one of the most prolific agricultural producing areas in the state.

At the turn of the century Solano county was known as the "Orchard of America." In the 1920s stiff competition from rivals in the central valley resulted in a decline of Solano's orchard industry. They still play a big role in the county's economic and cultural health even though urban growth has reduced their yield.

BROCCOLI CHEESE SALAD

SERVES 6–8
Submitted by Tom Thompson - cookbook photographer

4 - cups broccoli, cut up
1 - medium red onion, sliced into rings
1 - 6 oz box button mushrooms, sliced
2/3 - cup mozzarella cheese, cubed
(or extra firm tofu cubed)
1/3 - cup Bac-O's
(or crumbled crisp bacon optional)
Italian salad dressing (for marinade)

DRESSING:
1/4 - cup granulated sugar
3/4 - cup low fat mayonnaise
3 - Tablespoons red wine vinegar

1 Cut cheese (or tofu) into 1/2" cubes and marinate for a couple of hours or overnight in zesty Italian salad dressing.

2 Use only the flower parts of the broccoli and quarter them into small bite sizes. Slice the red onion with that State Fair slicer into separated rings about 1/4 inch thick. Rinse the mushrooms, dry and mix with broccoli and onion rings. Make the dressing and spoon it over the mix of broccoli, mushrooms and red onion. Be gentle. Pour just enough to lightly coat the veggies. Pour excess Italian dressing off the mozzarella cheese. Add cheese and Bac-O's to salad and mix thoroughly. Serve immediately. Do not add dressing ahead of time. ✣

AG PERFUME

Isn't it true that when your thoughts turn to the heartland your first sense of recall is the smell? Call it odor or essence, the identifiable, undeniable perfume of the farm or ranch is unforgettable and stays with us forever.

It catches in your nostrils at dusk as you wander through the heartland. It's that cool breath of damp alfalfa.

It's the musty incense that wafts from a barn in the first dust kicked up in the morning.

It's the nectar in the air as you travel the Blossom Trail in spring.

Even water takes on the fragrance of the heartland as it slakes the thirst of dry acreage.

The scent of freshly turned soil implies new life for productive land lending a hint of optimism from the bouquet of the heartland.

BEEF TENDERLOIN WITH PEPPER CRUST

SERVES 4–6

Submitted by Ann Veneman, Former Secretary, California Department of Food & Agriculture

2 1/2 lbs - beef tenderloin roast
2 - Tablespoons extra virgin olive oil (for rubbing)
1/2 - cup cracked black peppercorns (or more)
1 - cup Mushroom Ragout (see recipe below)
1 - bunch fresh parsley (for garnish)
1 - red bell pepper (for garnish)
1 - small box cherry tomatoes (for garnish)

1 Preheat oven to 450 degrees.

2 Remove all visible fat from tenderloin roast. Rub the entire surface of roast with olive oil. Press cracked pepper generously into the roast—cover completely, creating a crust. Place aluminum foil in bottom of roasting pan to make cleanup easier. Place roast in pan and lower the oven to 350 degrees. Use a meat thermometer to determine desired level of doneness. Roast to an internal temperature of 130 degrees for rare (about 15 minutes per pound). Cook longer for medium-rare. When it reaches your favorite level of doneness, remove from the oven and let rest for a few minutes.

3 Carve in 1/2" slices. Arrange on a platter garnished with fresh parsley, cherry tomatoes and small slices of red bell peppers. Pour Mushroom Ragout sauce over roast slices before serving. ✣

MUSHROOM RAGOUT

Submitted by Ann Veneman, Former Secretary, California Department of Food & Agriculture

1/3 lb - each of Portabella, Cremini and Oyster mushrooms
2 - Tablespoons butter
1/4 - cup dry white wine
salt and pepper to taste

1 Wash and slice mushrooms. Melt butter in a large skillet. Saute mushrooms for a few minutes until they create liquid. Add the dry white wine, salt and pepper to taste. Serve over roast and steamed white rice. ✣

CALIFORNIA BLESSING

In California, traditions from other cultures have become established. When I was ten or eleven, an Armenian friend and his family took me to their community's annual Blessing of the Grapes. Mounds of green and red grape bunches were piled high on a large table. A priest walked by and swept his hand over them while making the sign of the cross. He prayed aloud in Armenian. My friend's mother translated, "He prays for good weather and the strength to see us through the harvest."

The farmers in the audience took this ritual very seriously, believing a good harvest counted on the success of this ceremony. Their eyes dropped to the ground, heads bowed before the juicy clusters. Afterwards we all received a bunch of grapes. I munched the berries and felt as if I had received a communion.

When I came home, I asked Dad if Japanese practice such a ritual.

"I don't think grapes were grown very much in Japan," he said.

"I guess we need to rely on the Armenians to help bless our raisins for all the rest of us," I concluded. "We'll just have to depend on each other to get this harvest in."

—David Mas Masumoto
Excerpt from *"Harvest Son Planting Roots in American Soil"*

CALIFORNIA QUESADILLAS

SERVES 4

Submitted by Michele Anna Jordan‡

8 - large flour tortillas
3 - cups St. George cheese or Monterey jack, shredded or crumbled
2 - Tablespoons torn cilantro leaves
Mexican style hot sauce or salsa
guacamole (see recipe below)

1 Heat griddle or large frying pan; warm tortillas, one at a time on both sides. Return one of the tortillas to the pan. Distribute one quarter each of the fresh cilantro leaves and cheese on top and top with another tortilla. Cook until the cheese is almost completely melted (about 4 minutes). Turn and cook for 1 to 2 minutes more, until the cheese is completely melted. Cook the remaining quesadillas in the same manner. Cut each quesadilla into 6 triangles and serve immediately with hot sauce or salsa and guacamole. ✣

MARTY'S MEXICAN GUACAMOLE

Submitted by Marty Martinez

4 - ripe avocados
1/2 - small red onion, finely chopped
5 - Tablespoons medium or hot salsa
5 - Tablespoons sour cream (fat free)
1 - lemon, juiced
1/2 - teaspoon cumin
1/4 - teaspoon cayenne pepper (or to taste)
1/2 - teaspoon Mexican seasoning
Tabasco sauce, a dash optional

1 Mash avocados in medium bowl, add finely diced onion and about 5 Tablespoons of salsa of your temperature choice. Add 5 heaping Tablespoons of sour cream. Remove seeds from lemon and squeeze 1/2 of lemon juice into mixture. Add the next 3 spices to taste. Mix together well. Sprinkle top with lemon to preserve and keep the color. Place a hefty dollop on each quesadilla and use it with tortilla chips as a dip. ✣

MISSION FARMS

Hundreds of years ago, the Spaniards gave us something that would one day make the state of California not only one of the most self-sufficient, but one of the single largest economies in the world. What they gave us was farming.

Father Junipero Serra is considered the father of the mission system in California. Father Serra found the Mediterranean climate perfect for growing crops native to Spain.

One of the goals of the missions was to make the inhabitants self sufficient. Tomatoes, figs, pears, apricots, peaches, walnuts, almonds and other important agricultural products have their literal roots in California's missions.

Father Serra founded nine of the twenty-one missions in the state, walking thousands of miles up the California coast spreading not only the seeds of Christianity, but also the seeds of agriculture.

‡ Reprinted from *California Home Cooking* by Michele Anna Jordan, Copyright © 1997, with permission from Harvard Common Press, 535 Albany Street, Boston, MA 02118, 888-657-3755

FLOWER POWER

California can take credit for discovering gold and even giving birth to the computer industry. But the state can also lay claim to establishing the cut flower industry in the West.

Our Mediterranean climate and a Ventura housewife, Theodosia Shepherd can share the honor of giving birth to the industry. Ms. Shepherd started selling the flowers she raised in her garden back in the 1870s. Soon other women began selling their flowers and before long a florist profession was born.

California grows a wide variety of cut flowers, partly because of the climate, but also because of an advanced greenhouse technology

The flower growers of the heartland produce 60 percent of all domestically grown and commercially sold flowers in the nation.

CHICKEN ARTICHOKE CACCIATORE

SERVES 4

Submitted by Nir Weinblut - Jewish Family Services

1 - 3 lb fryer, cut up or 4 breasts, halved
2 - 6 oz jars marinated artichoke hearts
2 - Tablespoons olive oil
flour for dredging
1 - can (1lb) Italian solid pack tomatoes, include the juice
2 - garlic cloves, minced
1/2 - pound fresh mushrooms, sliced
1/2 - teaspoon salt
1/2 - teaspoon dry oregano
1/4 - cup fresh basil, chopped coarse
1/2 - teaspoon freshly ground pepper
1/4 - cup dry sherry or fine dry marsala
1 - bunch fresh parsley, chopped

1 Drain marinade from artichoke hearts into a large skillet and add olive oil. Dredge chicken in flour and brown in oil until golden. Transfer chicken pieces from skillet into a 3 quart casserole.

2 In a skillet combine whole can of tomatoes and juice, artichoke hearts, garlic, mushrooms and spices. Stir over low heat for 15 minutes to cook down and blend flavors. Pour over chicken. Cover and bake at 350 degrees for 1 hour or until tender. During the last 5 minutes pour wine over chicken and let simmer. Garnish with parsley. Serve with seasoned risotto. ✣

CHICKEN CREOLE

SERVES 4

Submitted by Patrick Celestin of Celestin's Caribbean Restaurant

CHICKEN MARINADE:
2 - teaspoons Worcestershire sauce
1/2 - teaspoon salt
1/2 - teaspoon cayenne pepper
1/2 - teaspoon garlic minced
1/2 - teaspoon freshly ground black pepper
4 - Tablespoons fresh lemon juice
4 - boneless chicken breasts (leave skin on)

CREOLE SAUCE:
2 1/4 - cups chicken stock
1 3/4 - cups finely diced onions
1 - Tablespoon garlic, minced
1 - small red bell pepper (grind fine in food processor - don't puree)
1 - medium size carrot (grind fine in food processor)
1 - 6 oz can tomato paste
3/4 - cup tomatoes, diced
2 - Tablespoons dark brown sugar
1 - Tablespoon black pepper
1 - Tablespoon allspice*
1/2 - teaspoon salt
1 - teaspoon thyme
1/3 - cup olive oil

CHICKEN MARINADE:

1 Mix together all ingredients except the lemon juice. Sprinkle lemon juice on 4 boneless chicken breasts and pound gently until they are an even thickness. Sprinkle all other ingredients onto chicken and blend with fingers. Place chicken in a plastic bag and refrigerate overnight.

CREOLE SAUCE:

2 Saute onions until translucent. Add garlic and cook until golden. Add tomatoes, carrots and red bell pepper. Cook over medium heat for 5 to 7 minutes. Add all spices and mix well. Add 2 cups chicken stock, bring to boil for 5 minutes and add remaining onion.

ASSEMBLE:

3 Dust chicken with flour. Heat 2 Tablespoons oil in 9" skillet. Place marinated chicken skin side down and saute until brown. Turn chicken over and discard oil. Add 3/4 cup Creole sauce and 1/4 cup chicken broth. Boil down over medium heat to thicken sauce. Place chicken on plate skin side up. Reduce sauce a bit more then pour over chicken. Serve with steamed white rice. ✣

*SECRET INGREDIENT = allspice

REALLY FARM FRESH

Every day, at pushcarts, roadside stands, and farmer's markets, consumers are making a connection with the bountiful harvest of California's heartland at its most elemental level—direct from the farmer. They are celebrating the fruits of their own region, learning how their food is produced and who their farmers are. All across the state, the markets—from the smallest cart to the world-famous Los Angeles Farmer's Market (3,000,000 visitors each year!)—are flourishing, keeping farms alive, and offering shoppers a tremendous variety of top-quality tree- and vine-ripened produce at reduced prices. Farmer's markets are community gathering places, alive with activity and rich in sensory experiences—sights, smells, and sounds that stimulate centers of our brain left dormant by supermarket shopping.

—Jim O'Donnell

FARMING FUTURE

"We do everything hands-on. I've done artificial insemination classes, welding classes. We've bought stocks on the computer, been in the market doing that. I'm going to a seminar on how to grow crops on the moon. So if I'm going to learn how to grow crops on the moon, there's basically no limitations."
—Rosealee Livorsi, Student

As California's agriculture industry starts a new century, still growing, still producing much of what the world needs, it is prudent to ask: "How can we sustain the success the heartland has achieved?"

Today's students, who will be the farmers of the future will have to know more about science and engineering. They will understand world business markets and will know how to travel in that heady atmosphere of international trade.

California's schools are preparing a bright new crop of not just farmers, but agricultural specialists.

CARROT FRITTERS

SERVES 4
Submitted by Michele Anna Jordan ‡

Peanut oil for deep frying
4 - cups carrots, peeled and grated
1/4 - cup cilantro leaves, minced
1 - teaspoon fresh ginger, grated
2 - teaspoons cumin seed, toasted and crushed
1 - Tablespoon white mustard seeds
4 - Tablespoons all-purpose flour
2 - teaspoons baking powder
1 - teaspoon salt
1 - teaspoon freshly ground black pepper
4 - eggs, lightly beaten
1 - large bunch cilantro, broken into sprigs
Honey Ginger Mustard Dipping Sauce **(see recipe on page 57)**

1 In a deep frying pan, (12" cast iron skillet) heat about two inches of peanut oil to 350 degrees.

FRITTER BATTER:

2 While the oil is heating, quickly mix the fritter batter. In a large mixing bowl, toss together the grated carrots, minced cilantro and ginger. In a small bowl, combine the cumin, mustard seeds, flour, baking powder, salt and pepper. Add the mixture to the carrots and toss together lightly. Pour the beaten eggs over the carrot mixture and toss with a fork just to combine.

TO MAKE FRITTERS:

3 All ingredients are now thoroughly mixed in one bowl. Use a small 1 oz ice cream scoop or a soup spoon to shape the fritters. Drop them one by one into the hot oil, being careful not to crowd them. Turn the fritters after 1 minute and fry until they are golden brown—about 1 minute more. Using a slotted spoon, transfer the fritters to absorbent paper to drain. Hold each batch in a warm oven until you are ready to serve. Allow the oil to return to 350 degrees before adding each new batch of fritters. Spread cilantro sprigs on a serving platter, place the fritters on top and serve immediately with honey ginger mustard sauce on the side. ✣

IN FRONT OF THE PLOW

They somehow seem bigger than life and are often referred to as the "Gentle Giants." They are called Clydesdales, Perchons, Belgians, Suffolks and yes, mules.

They are draft animals that so ably brought us into the age of mechanized agricultural technology and then were often dismissed to an uncertain future.

The draft horses' place in agricultural history was nearly wiped out thanks to the technological revolution.

One breed that was almost eradicated is the rare Suffolk. Reportedly there were only five or six of the breed remaining in the world at one time.

The annual Draft Horse Classic in Grass Valley is a wonderful mix of beauty and brawn. It is a gathering of devoted horse lovers with just one purpose, honoring the breed.

CHOCOLATE PORT CAKE

SERVES 4
Submitted by Christopher Mariscotti of The Vineyard - Madera

1 - cube (1/2 cup) unsalted butter
1/2 - cup Ficklin Port wine
4 oz - unsweetened chocolate
1 - cup granulated sugar
3 - eggs, separated
3/4 - cup all-purpose flour, sifted
1/8 - teaspoon salt

1 Use one 10" cake pan. Line bottom of pan with wax paper, butter, then dust with flour. Melt together in a double boiler, wine, butter, and chocolate. Set aside 2 Tablespoons of sugar. Combine remaining sugar and egg yolks in a mixer and beat until pale yellow. Add melted chocolate slowly so it will not cook the eggs. Beat until smooth, then add flour and salt and beat until smooth again. Beat egg whites and sugar until soft peaks form. When the whites are firm, fold in 1/3 of the chocolate mixture.

2 Transfer to a clean bowl and fold in remaining chocolate. Pour batter into the cake pan. Bake for 30 minutes in a 325 degree oven. Best served warm. This cake may be served as a one layer cake topped with sauce or as a two layer cake with frosting. ✣

CHOCOLATE PORT SAUCE

Submitted by Christopher Mariscotti of The Vineyard - Madera

1 - cup granulated sugar
1/4 - cup Ficklin Port wine
2 - cups water
8 oz - unsweetened chocolate
1/4 - cup heavy cream

1 Boil water, sugar and wine to make a syrup. Reduce heat, melt chocolate. Remove from heat and add cream. Pour warm sauce over cake and serve with a generous scoop of vanilla ice cream. ✣

EXCELLENT EXTRA = To give this cake a Christmas holiday spin, add to the cake recipe an extra 1/2 cup of very finely chopped dried Bing cherries or cranberries soaked overnight in 1/2 cup of Port wine.

CAIRNS CORNER

John Cairns is the keeper of Cairns Corner, an oasis of agricultural produce and agrarian history. The Cairns name is linked to the development of farming in Tulare County and the establishment of Lindsay as the olive capital of California. The Mission variety olive trees planted by John's great-great grandfather, J.J. Cairns in 1894 still shade Cairns Corner on Highway 65. The trees which now range from 40 to 60 feet tall, were originally planted as a windbreak. But, they were also productive to the tune of 62 tons of olives which brought $55 a barrel in 1907. If you doubt the importance of this intersection of our agricultural past, the transportation department is re-routing highway improvement around the old stand of trees, treating them as historical landmarks.

DEEP ROOTS

Though most people don't recognize them as such, our forests are also part of California's agricultural profile.

Thirty-seven million acres of the over 100-million acres of land mass in the state is made up of forests. Redwoods, Ponderosa Pine, White Fir, Sugar Pine, Douglas Fir and incense cedar. Soft woods that go toward providing the basic ingredient for everything from the chair you sit on, this book you're reading and the tires on your car.

It's as cyclical as any farming operation, though the crop is bulkier and takes years to yield. The demand for the products our forests provide will grow by 50 percent by the year 2020.

It's easy to get swept up in the beauty of our forests. No one knows that better than the people who harvest them and those who fight to conserve them.

CRAB LINGUINE

SERVES 4
Submitted by Michele Anna Jordan ‡

1 lb - linguine pasta (package)
2 - Tablespoons butter
2 - cloves garlic, crushed
1 - Tablespoon Tobasco sauce
1 - fresh crab, (about 1/2 pound) cooked and removed from shell
1 - bunch fresh Italian parsley, torn apart

1 Cook 1 lb linguine pasta according to package directions. In a small skillet, melt 2 Tablespoons butter. Add 2 cloves crushed garlic and sizzle in butter. Add 1 Tablespoon Tobasco sauce to melted butter. Pour half of the garlic butter over the cooked linguine and toss. Add the meat from 1 crab and toss again. Toss the crab legs in the remaining garlic butter and scatter over the top. Sprinkle with Italian parsley and lemon. Serve with Italian garlic bread (see recipe below.) ✣

ITALIAN GARLIC BREAD

SERVES 4
Submitted by Michele Anna Jordan ‡

1 - loaf Italian bread
1 - cube (1/2 cup) butter
3 - cloves garlic, pressed
Parmesan cheese, grated

1 Split one loaf of Italian bread down the middle the long way. In a small microwave-safe bowl, melt butter. Add garlic. Melt in microwave until fully liquid. With a pastry brush, paint the garlic butter liberally on both halves of the bread. Sprinkle on plenty of freshly grated Parmesan cheese.

2 Place under oven broiler until bread is slightly brown around the edges and butter is bubbly. Remove from oven. Slice into 1 1/2" sections and serve immediately. ✣

CRABBY SEAFOOD CAKES

SERVES 4
Submitted by Heidi Cusick - Mendocino

1 - jumbo egg
1/4 lb - fresh crab meat
1/4 lb - shrimp, peeled, deveined and coarsely chopped
1/3 lb - rock fish or salmon fillet, coarsely chopped
2 - sea scallops, chopped (optional)
2 - green onions, finely chopped
1/2 - cup red and green bell peppers, finely chopped
1 - teaspoon dry mustard
salt and freshly ground black pepper to taste
3 - Tablespoons fresh parsley, finely chopped
1/2 - cup fine dried bread crumbs
4 - Tablespoons olive oil

1 In a mixing bowl, beat the egg. Add the seafood, green onions, bell peppers, mustard, salt and pepper. Stir in parsley and enough bread crumbs to hold the mixture together. Form into 4 large patties. An empty tuna can with top and bottom removed makes a perfect mold to form patties. Dust with more bread crumbs.

2 In a large skillet, heat the olive oil. Place the empty tuna can (both ends removed) in the skillet. Pack the crab cake mixture firmly. Leave the mold in place while you fry the first side. Remove mold and turn the patties over. Fry the patties until browned on each side and cooked through—about 10 minutes total.

3 Serve with a mild tarter sauce and lemon wedges. ✣

AQUACULTURE

A growing population has sparked efforts to expand our food resources in the heartland. There is a renewed interest in harvesting the sea and establishing fish farms throughout the state.

In Monterey, after a dry spell, they are once again harvesting the sardine, rekindling memories of Steinbeck's Salinas Valley and Cannery Row.

From Alaska to the Baja Peninsula the Pacific Blue Mussel is a favorite, a healthy ingredient in main dishes, salads and appetizers.

Northern Californians tout Pacific crab fresh from San Francisco's Fisherman's Wharf.

Whether aquafarming from the sea or fresh water, the aquafarming industry is making a big splash in diet-conscious California.

AG RAILROAD

Spirits of the movers and shakers of our agricultural history can be found in pastures throughout the heartland, living in the remnants of ancient ag machinery. The railroad was part of that history. All kinds of produce has been shipped on the rails. Everything from apricots to artichokes.

It's hard to imagine how many rail cars have snaked through the Salinas Valley and along the central coast carrying harvests from the salad bowl and the sea.

Refrigerated rail cars changed the face of agriculture in the heartland allowing produce to be shipped farther and faster and to arrive fresher.

CHICKEN ENCHILADAS

SERVES 4

Submitted by Carol Laffranchi of Loleta Cheese Company

4 lb - whole chicken
1 - large onion (white or yellow)
1 - teaspoon garlic powder (or 1 garlic clove, minced)
1 - teaspoon onion salt
1 - teaspoon celery salt
salt and pepper to taste
2 - Tablespoons margarine
2 - Tablespoons shortening
1/4 - cup all-purpose flour
1 - Tablespoon chili powder (or to taste)
1/2 - teaspoon ground cumin
2 - cups cheddar cheese (sharp or mild), grated
12 - corn tortillas

CHICKEN:

1 Cook chicken with onion until tender. Pull apart into small pieces. Mix chicken with spices—garlic powder, onion salt, celery salt, salt and pepper. Set aside.

GRAVY:

2 In a 12" cast iron skillet, brown the flour in the margarine and shortening to make a roux (but don't let it burn). Add broth with onions to roux and blend until thick and bubbly. Add chili powder and cumin to taste. Add salt.

ASSEMBLE ENCHILADAS:

3 Soften corn tortillas over steam or place them one at a time in a heated skillet with a bit of melted butter for one minute—turning once. Stuff tortillas with chicken and roll. Place them in a greased 13" x 9" baking pan. Pour gravy mixture over enchiladas. Sprinkle grated cheese over top. Bake at 350 degrees for 15 to 20 minutes. Serve hot with salsa. ✣

CITRUS ALMOND SALAD

SERVES 4
Submitted by California Culinary Academy

DRESSING:
1/3 - cup orange juice
2 - Tablespoons white vinegar
2 - Tablespoons vegetable oil
1 - Tablespoon honey
2 - Tablespoons fresh grated ginger
1/4 - teaspoon salt
1/8 - teaspoon red pepper flakes

SALAD:
3 - naval oranges, sectioned
2 - red grapefruit, sectioned
1 - red onion, chopped
1 - bunch fresh spinach (baby leaves)
2/3 - cup slivered almonds, toasted

DRESSING:

1 Whisk together and set aside to chill.

SALAD:

2 Sprinkle sliced almonds on a cookie sheet in an even layer. Toast for no more than ten minutes in a 300 degree oven. Watch carefully and taste. Do not over toast as this will make the almonds bitter.

3 Wash and pat dry the raw spinach leaves. Pile leaves on individual plates. Spoon the citrus/onion mixture over the top. Add the dressing then garnish with toasted slivered almonds. ✣

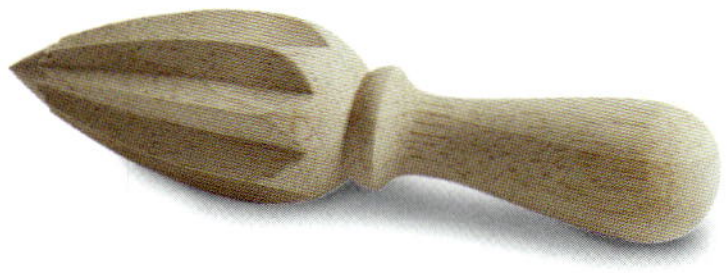

CITRUS REAMER

The citrus reamer is the perfect hand held tool for removing the juice from lemons, limes, and oranges without resorting to a conventional juice squeezer. Grasp one half of a citrus in one hand and squeeze as the other hand rotates the reamer in the center of the fruit.

CITRUS HERB MARINADE

Submitted by Lois Stanton for the May Herb Festival - San Diego County

1/2 - cup extra virgin olive oil
1/4 - cup fresh lemon juice
1 - clove garlic, finely chopped (or pressed)
2 - Tablespoons green onions, finely chopped
2 - Tablespoons grated lemon zest
2 - Tablespoons fresh basil and rosemary, chopped
1/2 - teaspoon salt
1/2 - teaspoon freshly ground black pepper

1 Whisk together all ingredients until thoroughly mixed.

2 Place in ziploc plastic bag with 4 skinned, boned, pounded chicken breasts. Turn bag with marinade and chicken periodically and refrigerate over night. Use marinade also to baste chicken during the barbecue process. ✣

CORITA'S APPLE BETTY

SERVES 6-8

Submitted by Corita Gravitt - California Heartland Executive Producer

5 - large sweet apples, unpeeled, cored and sliced
2/3 - cup all-purpose flour
1 - cube (1/2 cup) unsalted butter, room temperature
1/4 - cup granulated sugar
1/4 - cup dark brown sugar
1 - teaspoon cinnamon
1 - lemon, squeezed for juice
1/2 - cup raisins (or Sultanas - the small green ones)
1/2 - cup walnuts, chopped and lightly toasted

1 Preheat the oven to 350 degrees.

2 Mix sliced apples with raisins and walnuts. Lightly pile in a small glass 9" x 9" baking dish. Drizzle the apple mixture with a bit of lemon juice to prevent the apples from turning brown.

3 Mix together until crumbly, the flour, most of the softened butter, the sugar and cinnamon. Sprinkle 3/4 of the flour mixture over the apples and mix slightly. Before placing in the oven, sprinkle the remaining flour mixture on top and dot with remaining butter.

4 Bake for 35 minutes in a 350 degree oven, or until the mixture is nicely browned and apples are tender. Don't over bake. Serve warm by itself or with vanilla ice cream, or a great dollop of whipped cream. ✣

COUNTRY PEACH TART

SERVES 6-8
Submitted by Peter Van Konynenburg for Tri Valley Growers

1 - 32 oz jar S&W Growers Private Reserve cling peaches, drained; reserve the syrup from the canned peaches.
1/2 - cup raisins (try the green Sultanas for subtle color)
1 - Tablespoon cornstarch
3 - Tablespoons crystallized ginger, finely chopped
1/2 - teaspoon finely grated lemon peel (zest)
1 - 9" unbaked refrigerated pie crust
2 - Tablespoons finely ground almonds
2 - teaspoons granulated sugar
1/2 - teaspoon cinnamon
milk to brush on crust

1 Preheat oven to 425 degrees.

2 In a large bowl, blend together the cornstarch and 1 Tablespoon of the reserved peach syrup. Add peaches, raisins, crystallized ginger and lemon peel.

3 Lay pie crust on a lightly greased baking sheet. Blanch the almonds in boiling water for 3 minutes. Pop the skins off. Place them on a cookie sheet in a warm oven for at least 30 minutes to dry them out. Chop them coarsely in the food processor or blender. Combine ground almonds, sugar and cinnamon and sprinkle half this mixture on the pie crust.

4 Mound peach mixture in the center of the crust, leaving 1 1/2" border around the edge. Fold and pleat crust up and around the edge of filling, pinching and sealing cracks with a little water.

5 Brush crust with a little milk, sprinkle peaches with remaining nut mixture and bake at 425 degrees for 20 to 25 minutes or until the crust is golden.

6 Cool for at least 10 minutes before serving. Add your favorite ice cream, frozen yogurt or whipped cream. ✣

HITTING THE TRAILS

More and more Californians are hitting the trails, the Central Valley farm trails.

Farmers up and down the great valley are opening up their fields so visitors can get up close to the produce and the process, and even pick the choicest of their favorite fruits, vegetables or flowers.

In Stanislaus County "Just Tomatoes, Etc." in Westley encourages tourists to check out their six-thousand square foot processing plant.

Near Modesto the Fruit Barn of the Resendiz family represents a dream for a family that started out as farm workers over 30 years ago.

The farm trails concept is catching on as families and schools strive to learn more about the food we produce in California's heartland.

ODE TO COWS

Let's consider the contributions made by cows to the success of the heartland.

They must be important because many civilizations claim cows as gods. There was Achelous, a Greek river god who turned himself into a bull. Apis of Egypt was bull god of the sun. The Norsemen herald Audhumla the cow god.

Aside from their obvious value as beef, cheese and other dairy foods, there are other important byproducts produced from cows.

Out of a 1000-pound steer about 450 pounds of beef is garnered. But from that same cow can come ingredients that go toward making baseball gloves, buttons, cosmetics, glue, hydraulic brake fluid and hood ornaments.

EASY ONION RINGS

SERVES 4

Submitted by Chef Herve LeBiavant - California Culinary Academy

3 - large sweet onions (Walla Walla or Maui variety)
1/2 - cup yellow cornmeal
1/2 - cup all-purpose flour
1/2 - teaspoon salt
1/2 - teaspoon black pepper
3 - large eggs, beaten thoroughly
2 - cups peanut oil for frying

1 Slice onions into thin rings. (This is a good time to get out that magic slicer you bought at the State Fair several years ago.) Separate rings.

2 Preheat oil to 400 degrees in small deep fryer or cast iron skillet. Oil should be at least 1" deep.

3 Mix together the cornmeal, flour, salt and pepper in a pie pan. Drag each onion ring through the dry mixture. Dredge each ring in egg and drop into oil. Fry for approximately 30 seconds. Drain on paper towels placed on cookie sheets and season with additional salt and pepper. Serve immediately. ✣

FLOUR
ENRICHED
ALL PURPOSE
Pre-Sifted
NET WT. 2 LBS. (907g)
SALT

FRESH APPLE CAKE

SERVES 6-8

Submitted by Kathy Marcellino of David Berkley's Fine Wines & Specialty Foods

4 1/2 - cups raw apples, peeled and chopped
lemon juice to keep color
1 1/2 - cups salad oil
2 - cups granulated sugar
2 - large eggs
2 1/2 - cups all-purpose flour
1 - teaspoon salt
1 - teaspoon baking soda
2 - teaspoons baking powder
2 - teaspoons pure vanilla extract
1 1/2 - cups pecans, chopped and roasted

BUTTERMILK GLAZE:
2/3 - cup sugar
1/4 - teaspoon baking soda
1/3 - cup buttermilk
1/3 - cup unsalted butter
2 - teaspoons light corn syrup
1/2 - teaspoon pure vanilla extract

1 Prepare apples, use lemon juice to preserve color—set aside.

2 Add sugar and eggs to oil, mix well at low speed until creamy and smooth. Sift flour before measuring. Sift again with salt, baking soda and baking powder. Add flour mixture to creamed mixture a little at a time. Fold in well after each addition. Add vanilla. When the batter becomes stiff, remove beaters and finish mixing by hand. Fold in apples and nuts. Bake in a greased 9" x 13" pan 1 hour at 350 degrees. Check with toothpick for doneness or press lightly on cake to see if it springs back up. This is a very moist cake and so it will need the full baking time. Top with buttermilk glaze. Because of its moistness, this cake will stay fresh for days.

BUTTERMILK GLAZE:

3 Combine all ingredients except vanilla in a small saucepan. Bring to a boil and boil gently for 5 minutes. Add vanilla. Pour the glaze slowly over the cake and serve warm.

EXCELLENT EXTRA = To turn this into an autumn holiday cake you may add to the batter, 1 Tablespoon of ground cinnamon, and a 1/2 teaspoon each of ground cloves, freshly grated nutmeg and ground ginger.

RELICS

The names of "Case", "Holt", "Caterpillar" and "John Deere" grace antiquated and rusting relics of a heartland past; looking every bit like great machinery skeletons in burial grounds where they have come to die.

Some of the rusting carcasses were once the leading edge of agricultural technology that carried the country into the twentieth century. Many are on proud display at the unique Heidrick Ag History Center in Woodland, California.

How important were these devices of agriculture to the advancement of our culture? One report listed the mechanized reaper as the number one innovation in modern technology. The microprocessor is placed at number ten.

ARTICHOKE - SPINACH SALAD

SERVES 4–6
Submitted by Benjamin Ford of The Farm in Beverly Hills

4 - fresh artichokes
8 - cups fresh spinach
2 - Tablespoons walnut oil*
2 - Tablespoons extra virgin olive oil
2 - Tablespoons minced flat-leaf fresh parsley
1 - Tablespoon lemon juice
1 - Tablespoon orange juice
1/2 - Tablespoon lemon zest (grated rind)
1/2 - Tablespoon orange zest
1/2 - Tablespoon fresh thyme leaves
1/2 - teaspoon minced garlic
1 1/4 - cups chicken stock (use canned)
3 - Tablespoons unsalted butter
salt and pepper to taste

1 Combine all ingredients in a small bowl—except the butter, chicken stock, salt and pepper. In a saucepan reduce chicken stock by half, then whisk in butter. Whisk stock into vinaigrette. Season to taste.

ARTICHOKE:

2 Trim off all but the hearts of 4 fresh artichokes. Place them in one quart of boiling water into which you have added 3 Tablespoons fresh lemon juice and 1 teaspoon salt. Cover and reduce heat to simmer for 35 to 40 minutes or until hearts are tender when you spear them with a fork. Drain and rinse with cold water to stop cooking. Cut hearts in quarters.

SPINACH:

3 8 cups of young fresh spinach, cleaned and spin dry with your salad spinner. Toss the spinach with vinaigrette. Divide among four plates. Arrange artichoke hearts on spinach. Spoon on remaining vinaigrette. Sprinkle with seasoned bread crumbs. Serve immediately. ✣

*SECRET INGREDIENT = walnut oil

GINGERED BABY CARROTS

SERVES 4

Submitted by Ann Veneman, former Secretary, California Department of Food and Agriculture

1 lb - baby carrots, peeled
1 - Tablespoon of granulated sugar
1 - teaspoon cornstarch
1/4 - teaspoon ground ginger
1/4 cup orange juice
2 - Tablespoons butter
2 - Tablespoons chopped fresh parsley
salt to taste

1 Cook the baby carrots in lightly salted boiling water until they are slightly tender. Drain. In a small saucepan, thoroughly mix the cornstarch with a small amount of cold water so it won't lump, combine the sugar, ginger and salt. Add the orange juice, stirring constantly until the mixture thickens and bubbles. After boiling one minute, stir in the butter. Pour sauce over the carrots and toss to coat thoroughly. Garnish with the chopped parsley and serve immediately. ✣

THE FARMING WAY

Unless you've farmed it's hard to get a true picture of the rigors of the farmer's life. In Marin County you can get a taste of that lifestyle through a program developed by the Marin Agricultural Land Trust, or MALT. MALT's mission is to preserve Marin County farmland.

MALT excursions give participants a chance to get an up-close-and-personal view of what it takes to maintain a farm in the 21st century.

More than three-thousand people have taken advantage of the MALT experience. Hopefully they've come away with a deeper respect and understanding of just what it takes to bring the food to our table.

GILROY BRUSCHETTA

SERVES 6
Submitted by Christopher Ranch - Gilroy

8 - Roma tomatoes, chopped
4 - Tablespoons olive oil
2 - Tablespoons fresh basil, chopped
3 - cloves garlic, finely chopped or pressed
1/2 - cup fresh Romano cheese, shredded
salt and pepper to taste
1 - French bread baguette, sliced into 1/4" rounds

1 Lightly toast bread rounds on both sides under broiler until golden. Set aside. Combine tomatoes, oil, basil, garlic and cheese. Spread a spoonful of mixture on each bread slice. Garnish with one perfect whole basil leaf and serve. ✣

GARLIC PRESS

The garlic press is perhaps the most used hand tool in the kitchen. Peel the garlic and squeeze it through the press. Quick, simple and clean.

GREAT GARLIC SALAD DRESSING

Submitted by Corita Gravitt - California Heartland Executive Producer

1/4 - cup extra virgin olive oil
3 - cloves of garlic, minced (not pressed)
1/4 - teaspoon salt
1 - Tablespoon capers
1 - small can sliced black olives
black pepper to taste

1 Combine olive oil with garlic and salt and mix (or shake) well together. Let stand for a few minutes (or overnight) to let flavors blend. The salt binds the flavor of the garlic to the olive oil.

2 Select an appropriate bag of mixed Mediterranean salad greens, add one small can of sliced black olives (drained) and pour the dressing liberally over the mixture. Toss, give a couple of spins of freshly ground black pepper and serve. ✣

GRILLED ASPARAGUS WITH BELL PEPPERS

SERVES 4

Submitted by Jeff Mezzetta of Mezzetta & Co.

1 lb - fresh asparagus
1 - cup Mezzetta Roasted Yellow and Red Bell Peppers, sliced
1/2 - red onion, diced
2 - Tablespoons Mezzetta Imported Capers, drained
1/4 - cup fresh lemon juice
1/2 - cup Mezzetta Extra Virgin Olive Oil
salt and pepper to taste

1 Trim asparagus. Place on a hot grill. Brush lightly with Mezzetta Extra Virgin Olive Oil. Grill until wilted.

2 Meanwhile, saute onion in remaining olive oil, add Mezzetta Roasted Yellow and Red Bell Peppers and Mezzetta Imported Capers. Add lemon juice, salt and pepper to taste. Arrange asparagus on a platter, top with peppers and capers. Serve hot or cold. ✣

LABOR OF LOVE

My grandparents, Harriet and Manny Lund, were married for 61 years. As far back as I can remember, my grandmother would make Lemon Love Notes for my grandfather and the rest of our family. She then taught all of her grandchildren how to make these sweet treats. Whenever I would bake with her at her house, my grandfather would become the "official taste tester". He would always say, "I think I need to try just one more to make sure they're okay." Of course, this was just a way for him to indulge in another piece of this delectable dessert. This recipe was passed on to my grandmother by an acquaintance long ago, and ever since it has become a family tradition. Today, my grandmother, my mother, my sisters, and I continue to make Lemon Love Notes and always pass the recipe on for others to enjoy.

—Allison Thompson

LEMON LOVE NOTES

SERVES 6–8

Submitted by Allison Thompson, California Heartland producer/reporter, from her grandmother

CRUST:

1 - cup butter, at room temperature
2 - cups all-purpose flour, sifted
1/2 - cup powdered sugar, sifted

TOPPING:

4 - eggs, beaten
1/3 - cup fresh lemon juice (2 lemons)
2 - lemons zested
2 - cups granulated sugar
1/4 - cups all-purpose flour, sifted
1 - teaspoon baking powder

CRUST:

1 Mix together butter, 2 cups flour and powdered sugar by hand until they form into dough. Spread the dough onto an ungreased 13" x 9" baking pan. Bake for 15 minutes at 350 degrees or until golden brown. Check at 12 minutes. Remove from oven and cool in the baking pan.

TOPPING:

2 Blend all ingredients well for a few minutes with a hand mixer. Pour over the cooked crust once it has cooled.

3 Bake for 25 minutes and dust with powdered sugar. Cut into squares and serve with afternoon tea. ✣

ZEN & THE ART OF FARMING

Most heartland farmers are philosophical about the work they do but at the Green Gulch Farm the Zen philosophy is at the heart of their approach to how they work the land. Zen Buddhism is interwoven into the rhythms of daily life.

A Zen proverb states "a day without work is like a day without eating." In a cool fog belt in the San Francisco Bay Area Green Gulch produces beets and salad greens that help feed the Green Gulch community. The monks also supply farmers' markets and local stores.

Green Gulch is a thriving, working farm that has an aura of mystery about it. It's a blend of philosophy and farming where soil, seeds and soul are all nurtured to grow.

FRESH GREENS & RICE SOUP

SERVES 4

Submitted by Beverly Berkley of David Berkley's Fine Wine & Specialty Foods

5 - cups chicken stock
1/2 lb - fresh spinach leaves, julienned
1/2 lb - Swiss chard leaves, julienned
3 - Tablespoons extra virgin olive oil
4 - small cloves of garlic, peeled and minced
1 - Tablespoon ground cumin
2 - Tablespoons ground coriander seeds
2 - lemons, juiced and strained
salt and freshly ground black pepper to taste
1 - cup long grain basmati rice, cooked

1 Bring chicken stock to a boil in a medium saucepan over medium-high heat. Add greens, reduce heat to medium-low and simmer, allowing greens to dissolve into the stock—5 to 10 minutes.

2 Heat oil in a small skillet over medium heat. Add garlic and cook, stirring until fragrant—about 2 minutes. Stir in the cumin and coriander and continue to cook for 2 to 3 minutes.

3 Add garlic mixture to stock. Stir in the lemon juice and season with salt and pepper. Simmer until flavors blend—about 8 minutes.

4 Evenly divide the cooked rice among 8 bowls. Ladle soup over the rice and serve.

HONEY GINGER MUSTARD DIPPING SAUCE

Submitted by Michele Anna Jordan ‡

2 - Tablespoons hot dry mustard (such as Coleman's)
1 - Tablespoon ice water
3/4 - cup dijon mustard (Gray Poupon, of course)
1/4 - cup honey
1/4 - cup minced candied ginger
1 - teaspoon grated fresh ginger
2 - garlic cloves, finely minced (or pressed)
1/2 - teaspoon freshly ground black pepper
2 - Tablespoons fresh cilantro leaves, minced

1 Mix the dry mustard with the ice water in a small bowl to form a smooth paste. Let the paste stand for 20 minutes. Add the Dijon mustard, honey, candied and fresh ginger, garlic, pepper and cilantro. Stir until the mixture is smooth. Think about using your food processor or blender for the ultimate smoothness. Let the mustard rest for at least 30 minutes before using. Store covered in a glass jar in the refrigerator. ✣

HORSERADISH DIP

Submitted by Shelby Johnson

1 - cup low fat sour cream
1 - cup low fat mayonnaise
1/4 - cup creamed horseradish
1/4 - cup bacon bits (or Bac-O's if you're vegetarian)
1/4 - teaspoon dill weed

1 Mix all ingredients together thoroughly and chill. Serve with dipping corn chips or small crackers for this delicious dip that will bite back. ✣

‡ Reprinted from *California Home Cooking* by Michele Anna Jordan, Copyright © 1997, with permission from Harvard Common Press, 535 Albany Street, Boston, MA 02118, 888-657-3755

GARDEN COMMUNITIES

Not everyone has a green thumb. For many people, especially those in urban areas, the concept of farming or produce gardening is foreign. The idea of community gardens was a grass roots movement started as the world went to war.

The battles of World War II were fought on several fronts but a non-violent battle was being waged on the home front.

In California's heartland and throughout the country, individuals were fighting food shortages by establishing "Victory Gardens", small plots of vegetables and produce planted to bolster the war effort abroad.

When we sent the boys "over there" the country rallied around their efforts to win the war. The Victory Garden was one way Americans did their part.

The popularity of community gardens grew out of the Victory Garden program. Today the emphasis is on supplying healthy produce to inner city dwellers and training Master Gardeners.

LINGUINE BROCCOLINI

SERVES 4
Submitted by Mann Packing Company - Salinas

3/4 - cup butter
3 - Tablespoons all-purpose flour, sifted
2 - cups dry white wine
1 1/2 - cups light cream
1 - cup mini cherry tomatoes
2 1/2 - cups fresh basil leaves
1 - cup Mann's Broccolini*, cut into thirds, blanched 1 minute
1 - cup Romano cheese, coarsely grated
9 oz - fresh linguine

1 Drop Broccolini into a saucepan of boiling water. After 1 minute, drain and dip into cold water to stop cooking process. Drop linguine into saucepan of boiling water. Return to boil and cook 1 minute, if it's fresh, or according to package directions if it is dry. Check pasta for al dente doneness. Drain and toss with a little extra virgin olive oil.

SAUCE:

2 Melt butter. Whisk in flour to make a roux. Cook until bubbly. Whisk in wine and light cream and cook, stirring constantly until thickened. You may make the sauce ahead then reheat in the microwave.

ASSEMBLE:

3 When you are ready to serve, heat sauce to a boil in a large kettle. Add tomatoes and basil and cook 1 1/2 minutes or until limp. Add linguine and Broccolini and heat, stirring with a large wooden spoon until mixture is hot. Add cheese, heat through and season with salt and pepper to taste. Serve immediately with additional cheese and freshly ground pepper on top. ✣

*Broccolini is a tender new vegetable that is edible from flower to end of stem. Can be used raw in salads or lightly steamed for a unique vegetable course. Looks and feels like a tiny version of broccoli spears—but much sweeter. Ask your supermarket produce manager for this new product.

LINZERTORTE

SERVES 6-8

Submitted by Cate Conniff Dobrich of Culinary Institute of America

1 - cup hazelnuts (filberts), skinned and chopped
3 - cups cake flour
1 - teaspoon ground cinnamon
1 - teaspoon baking powder
1 - cup (2 sticks) unsalted butter, room temperature
3/4 - cup granulated sugar
1 - egg
1 - teaspoon vanilla extract
3/4 - cup seedless or sieved raspberry jam (18oz jar = 3/4 cup)
powdered sugar for dusting

1 Preheat oven to 350 degrees.

2 Butter and lightly flour a 10" round cake or tart pan with a nonremovable bottom.

3 To skin the hazelnuts, place them in a saucepan of boiling water and boil for 5 minutes. Remove from heat, run cold water over them. Squeeze gently and the skins will come off easily. Dry completely. In a blender or food processor, grind the nuts to a fine powder. If you cannot find hazelnuts you may substitute blanched and skinned almonds. Thoroughly dry them in a slow oven.

4 Sift together the cake flour, cinnamon and baking powder. Add the ground nuts to the sifted dry ingredients and set aside. In a large bowl, cream the butter and sugar together until smooth and fluffy. Mix in the egg and vanilla extract, scraping the sides of the bowl as necessary. Add the dry ingredients and mix until just incorporated. Do not over mix.

5 Spread half the mixture evenly over the bottom of the prepared pan. Spread the raspberry jam over the mixture to within 1/2" of the edge of the pan.

6 Transfer the remaining batter to a large pastry bag fitted with a No. 6 straight tip and pipe a lattice top. Pipe a shell border around the edge. Bake the cake for 45 to 50 minutes, or until the crust is crisp and browned. Check at 40 minutes for darkness of edge crust. If it is becoming too dark, place an aluminum foil collar just over the edge. Let cool completely. Dust with powdered sugar just before serving. Add a dollop of whipped cream or a scoop of ice cream to the serving plate. ✣

ONE SIZE FITS ALL

Large and small, all farms in the heartland produced an income of $24.5 billion in 1996. Almost a third of California's 100-million acres of land are in agricultural production.

According to the California Farm Bureau Federation the number of small farms has been dwindling across the nation. But thanks to California's cultural diversity, the niche markets they create, and the great weather, the movement of minority growers into the state has reversed this trend.

According to the Farm Bureau we eat about 2,175 pounds of food per person each year. That's about 900 calories more every day than the world-wide average.

Anyone like another rice cake?

VANISHING HEARTLAND

With images of the heartland's fertile ground burned into our consciousness, we should keep in mind that, according to the American Farmland Trust, the United States is losing 50 acres of prime agricultural land a day to the population explosion. California's heartland is at the top of the national list of endangered agricultural areas.

Beyond the neatly trimmed vineyards and blossoming orchards is the spectre of strip malls, split level homes and traffic.

Possible solutions run the gamut from establishing food belts around communities that would provide local food supplies and food sheds for larger urban areas, to building higher density housing.

In the Central Valley a coalition among business, conservation, agriculture and development groups has been formed to develop planning principles that will guide elected officials in adopting new patterns of urban growth.

MEDITERRANEAN VEGETABLE SALAD

SERVES 4

Submitted by Beverly Berkley of David Berkley's Fine Wines & Specialty Foods

2 - lbs fresh Roma tomatoes, diced large
1 - large English cucumber, seeded and diced
1 - medium red onion, diced
1/2 - lb baby spinach leaves
1 - cup Greek olives
1 - cup feta cheese, crumbled

DRESSING:
4 - Tablespoons champagne vinegar
6 - Tablespoons fresh lemon juice
2 - Tablespoons fresh mint leaves, finely chopped
4 - Tablespoons fresh oregano leaves, finely chopped
1/4 - teaspoon fresh garlic, chopped
1/2 - teaspoon salt
1/2 - teaspoon sugar
3/4 - cup olive oil
freshly ground black pepper to taste

1 Chop the Roma tomatoes and cucumber into small squares (large dice). Add the diced onion, baby spinach leaves, olives and feta cheese. Set aside.

2 Combine all the ingredients for the dressing. Add dressing to prepared vegetables and toss well. Serve at room temperature.

3 Serve with Gilroy Bruschetta (see recipe on page 50.)

HANDS

Let's consider the hands of the
Heartland; hands that coax and
nurture, steer and brand what comes
so neatly packaged.

Hands that cut and hew what comes
unbound from ground worked by hand.

Artichokes and apples,
broccoli and beans,
carrots and cauliflower,
and assorted greens.
Pears and peaches,
cattle feed,
flower seed and dates,
nectarines and tangerines
and varieties of grapes.

So easily we take for granted what
ends up on the world's table. Without
the hands of the heartland, it would
be a meager feast, at least.

LOW FAT CHILI POPPERS

SERVES 6

Submitted by Allison Thompson, California Heartland producer/reporter

15 - small green jalapeño peppers

BATTER:
1 - small box of cornbread mix
2 - egg whites
1/3 - cup non-fat milk

STUFFING:
3 - green onions, minced
1/2 - white onion, minced
3 - cloves garlic, chopped
1/2 - Tablespoon chili powder
1 - 8 oz package fat-free cream cheese, softened

STUFFING:

1 Wash 15 small green jalapeños and make a T-shaped slit on one side. Remove the seeds and rinse the inside thoroughly. Set aside.

2 Mix all of the stuffing ingredients together until well mixed. This will be the stuffing for the jalapeños chilies. A quick and easy way to do the stuffing would be to load the mix into a small pastry bag with a medium straight tip and pipe the stuffing into each pepper.

BATTER:

3 Combine the box of cornbread mix with two egg whites and 1/3 cup of non-fat milk. Mix well, then dip each of the stuffed peppers into the batter to coat evenly. Place on a lightly greased cookie sheet and bake for 20 minutes at 375 degrees. Let them cool slightly before serving. Place them on a platter garnished with cilantro leaves. ✣

MEXICAN POTATO SALAD

SERVES 6
Submitted by Michele Lites, Registered Dietitian

4 - large red potatoes
1/2 - cup low fat mayonnaise
3 - green onions, chopped
1 - stalk celery, chopped
1/2 - cup jicama, diced
1/2 - cup salsa
1/4 - cup Mexican corn
1/4 - cup low fat Monterey jack cheese

SEASONING:
1/2 - teaspoon chili powder
1/2 - teaspoon ground cumin
1/4 - teaspoon garlic powder
salt and pepper to taste
1 - lime, juice only

1 Boil potatoes until tender. Put them under cold water to stop the cooking process. Set them aside to cool. Dice potatoes into cubes. Assemble all other ingredients in a large bowl and mix. Add potatoes, mix and cover to refrigerate for at least one hour to blend flavors. ✣

MICHELE'S CAN-OPENER CHILE

SERVES 4
Submitted by Michele Lites, Registered Dietitian

2 - cans stewed tomatoes, chopped
2 - cans pork-n-beans (discard the fat pieces)
2 - cans black beans
2 - cans kidney beans
1 - medium onion, chopped coarsely
3/4 - cup thick BBQ sauce
2 - Tablespoons yellow mustard
2 - Tablespoons Mrs. Dash
2 - Tablespoons chili powder
2 - Tablespoons ground cumin
3 - cloves of garlic

1 Place all ingredients in a large crock-pot in the morning. Set on low heat and cook all day. Give it a stir once in a while to see how things are going and smelling. If you don't have a crock-pot, this recipe can be cooked on the stove for 20 minutes or until it is heated through. Just bring it up to a simmer and let it simmer for 20 minutes. Serve with Mexican cornbread and some of those low fat chili poppers. It doesn't get easier than this! ✣

SECRET INGREDIENT = can opener

AG PHENOMENON

California is truly a phenomenon with its more than 250 commodities ranging from almonds to zucchini. Our farmers and ranchers are extremely proud of the endless variety of food, fiber and flowers that we produce.

The word "California" connotes quality around the world. People in other countries are willing to pay a large premium for our products because they know they will be getting quality. That reputation comes form the dedication of the men and women who till the soil from El Centro to Yreka.

Farm Bureau is pleased to be a "founding sponsor" of California Heartland. We appreciate the opportunity to tell the story of California agriculture to the 99 percent of the people in California who live off the farm but share in the bounty of our industry. We are proud of the work that is done by farmers and ranchers in producing quality products while supporting the environment and providing nearly one in ten California jobs.

Welcome to the Heartland!

—Bill Pauli, President
California Farm Bureau Federation

CHAMPAGNE ANYONE?

There was a French Benedictine monk named Dom Perignon. They say he had a brilliant mind but an even keener sense of smell. He recognized that a particular type of white wine, Ay of Champagne, would become effervescent with a second fermenting. He also invented the mushroom shaped cork and wire cage that lets the sparkling wine be bottled safely.

The bubbles in champagne develop during the fermenting process. Carbon dioxide is produced. When you ferment wine in a closed container, like a bottle, the gas is trapped. When you pop Monsieur Perignon's cork the gas comes out.

Be aware that when that cork is popped it becomes a missile traveling close to 65 mph. Make sure you choose a trajectory away from friends and family.

MUSHROOM "PESTO" RAGOUT

Submitted by Ann Veneman, Former Secretary, California Department of Food & Agriculture

1 lb - mushrooms (combinations of Cremini, Portabella and Oyster)
2 - Tablespoons butter
2 - cloves garlic, finely minced (or pressed)
1/2 - cup fresh basil leaves, finely chopped
1/4 - cup dry white wine
salt and pepper to taste

1 Wash and slice the mushrooms. Melt two tablespoons of butter in a large skillet. Add garlic and basil leaves and saute for about 2 minutes. Add the mushrooms and continue to saute for a few minutes, until they begin to generate liquid. Add the dry white wine, salt and pepper to taste. Continue to simmer for an additional 3 minutes. Perfect for serving over a plate of pasta or cooked beef in any form. ✣

MINT FLAVORED ICE CREAM

Submitted by Steve Albaugh - peppermint grower

4 - eggs
2 1/4 - cups sugar
1/2 - teaspoon salt
5 - cups milk
4 - cups heavy cream
2 - Tablespoons peppermint extract
1 - cup small chocolate chips
4 - drops of green food coloring

1 Beat eggs in mixer until foamy. Add sugar and salt and continue to beat until stiff. Add milk, cream, peppermint flavoring, 4 drops of green food coloring and the chocolate chips. Stir together with the rubber spatula (not the mixer) until thoroughly combined. This mix is now ready for your freezer. Fill ice trays without the dividers and place in the freezer. If you have the old fashioned hand crank freezer, ice and salt it up then turn the crank until you can no longer turn it. Serve immediately with sprigs of mint leaves and plates of chocolate chip cookies. ✣

ONION FESTIVAL RICE

SERVES 4

Submitted by Marjorie King, author 'The Road Home"

2 - Tablespoons extra virgin olive oil
1 - large red onion, chopped
4 - celery ribs, chopped
1/4 lb - fresh mushrooms, sliced
2 - cups chicken broth
1 - cup rice
1 - Tablespoon fresh parsley, chopped
2 - Tablespoons fresh sage leaves, finely chopped
1 - Tablespoon fresh rosemary leaves, chopped
1 - Tablespoon fresh thyme leaves, chopped
1/2 - teaspoon salt
freshly ground black pepper

1 Heat the oil in a 1 quart saucepan (or larger). Add chopped onions and saute just until they begin to turn brown. Stir in celery, stir and cook for 1 minute. Add mushrooms, rice, finely chopped parsley, sage, rosemary, thyme, salt and pepper. Mix thoroughly. Pour broth over the mixture. Bring it to a boil. Stir lightly and cover the pan. Lower the heat and simmer for 20 minutes. The liquid should disappear and the rice should be fluffy as you stir it with a fork. Remove from heat and allow to sit (covered) for at least five minutes before serving. ✣

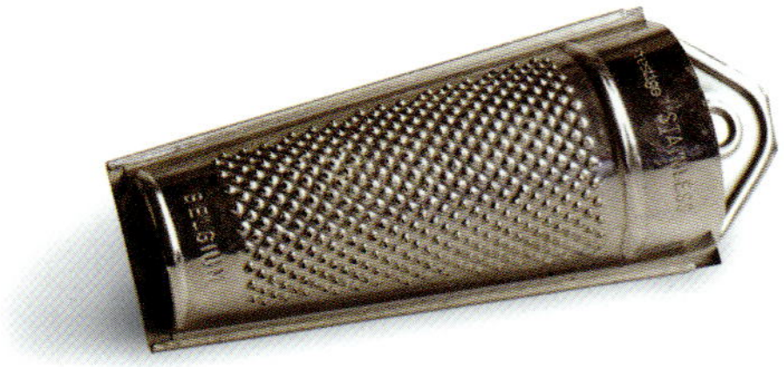

NUTMEG GRATER

The nutmeg grater is specific to that task. When the recipe calls for freshly grated nutmeg, this is the only tool that can do the job.

MOCK MASHED POTATOES

SERVES 6

Submitted by Michele Lites, Registered Dietitian

1 - package (10 oz) frozen cauliflower*
(or 1 medium cauliflower head)
2 - Tablespoons low fat milk
1 - teaspoon instant chicken bouillon
1/4 - teaspoon butter flavored salt
(Butter Buds)
dash of freshly ground pepper
salt to taste
a whisper of freshly ground nutmeg*

1 Place cauliflower in a 1 quart casserole dish. Cover with plastic wrap. Microwave on high for 8 to 10 minutes or until the cauliflower is very tender. Drain off water. Place in a food processor. Add milk a bit at a time so the puree doesn't become too liquid. Then add the bouillon, butter substitute and pepper. Blend until smooth, three to five minutes. Taste, then add salt if needed. You may want to serve with a low fat brown gravy. ✣

This dish has only 21 calories per serving and 0.2 grams of fat. Make them taste it before you tell them what it is! It will look and taste exactly like real mashed potatoes.

*SECRET INGREDIENTS = cauliflower and nutmeg

PACIFIC SALMON AND VEGETABLES

SERVES 4–6

Submitted by the California Salmon Council

MARINADE:

1/3 - cup olive oil
3 - Tablespoons balsamic vinegar
3 - Tablespoons seasoned rice wine vinegar
1 - Tablespoon Dijon mustard
2 - cloves garlic, crushed
1/2 - teaspoon salt
1/4 - teaspoon coarsely ground black pepper
1/4 - teaspoon crushed red pepper
4 - 6 oz Pacific salmon fillets

VEGETABLES:

3/4 lb - (about 4 cups) broccoli florets with 2 1/2" stems
1 - cup Roma tomatoes, diced
1/3 - cup red onion, diced
2 - Tablespoons capers
2 - Tablespoons fresh basil leaves, chopped
2 - Tablespoons fresh dill, chopped
Balsamic marinade

MARINADE:

1 In a small bowl, whisk together oil, vinegars, mustard, garlic, salt, black and red pepper. Remove 1/4 cup marinade to baste salmon while grilling or broiling. Remainder of marinade is for the vegetables.

VEGETABLES:

2 Steam broccoli about 5 minutes or until crisp-tender. Rinse with cold water to stop cooking process. Place in large bowl with tomatoes, onions, capers, basil and dill. Pour remainder of marinade over the vegetables in bowl and marinate.

ASSEMBLE:

3 Grill or broil four 6 oz California Pacific Salmon fillets and serve over room temperature vegetables. ✣

TAKING THE LEAD

"California is going to continue to play a major role. For the state to do that they have to continue to work on the problem of preserving the agriculture in California.

There is more interest and awareness in making sure that we protect what is really some of the last Mediterranean climate agricultural production area in the world; where we can produce crops that can be produced in few other places in the world."

—Richard Rominger
Deputy Secretary, USDA

According to the California Department of Agriculture, it's going to take the diligence of every California resident if the state is going to continue its leadership role in the world of agriculture.

Ask almost anyone affiliated with agriculture what the future holds and most will tell you it is "crunch" time for nearly every aspect of the industry.

WATER WATCH

By the year 2010 Californians will be using four percent more water than they use today. So claims the California Department of Water Resources. What does that mean for heartland farmers?

The agriculture industry is bracing for some difficult challenges. There is a three way tug-of-war going on between urban, agricultural and environmental interests over who gets how much water, and when.

All sides agree further damage to the environment must be stopped and urban growth is necessary. All the factions have water needs and heartland farmers are fearful that badly needed water will be diverted from thirsty crops.

So the pressure is on; more water for more people; a stable supply for crops; good quality water for habitat and animals. Let's hope Mother Nature doesn't conjure up another drought.

PEPPER CRUSTED SALMON

SERVES 4

Submitted by the California Salmon Council

4 - 6 oz fresh California King Salmon fillets
1/4 - cup peppercorns, mixed red, green and black, lightly crushed
1/2 - teaspoon coriander seeds, crushed
1/3 - cup sunflower oil

1 Rinse salmon fillets and set aside. Combine crushed peppercorns and coriander seeds in a shallow pan. Mix well. Press the mixture gently into the salmon fillets. In a heavy fry pan, heat the sunflower oil until it is very hot. Place fillets pepper-side down in the hot oil. Saute until peppers and salmon are nicely browned. Turn fillets and finish cooking. Serve immediately with a generous garnish of fruit salsa (see recipe below.) ✣

FRUIT SALSA

Submitted by the California Salmon Council

1 - Tablespoon rice wine vinegar
1 - Tablespoon apple cider vinegar
1 - Tablespoon water
2 - teaspoons granulated sugar
2 - Tablespoons red onion, coarsely diced
1 - each fresh ripe plum, nectarine and peach, pit and dice
1 - green onion, thinly sliced
1 - firm, ripe Roma tomato, peeled, seeded and finely diced
1/2 - teaspoon red pepper flakes
salt and pepper to taste

1 Combine vinegar, water and sugar in a saucepan and bring to a boil, stirring until the sugar is all dissolved. Add onion and return to boil. Remove from heat and let stand for about 10 minutes. Drain onion, reserving brine. Let cool. In a small mixing bowl, combine pickled onion, fruit, green onion, tomato and 1 1/2 Tablespoons of the brine. Sprinkle with red pepper flakes. Salt and pepper to taste. Refrigerate before using. ✣

AG ENVIRONMENT

One of the great challenges heartland farmers struggle with is how to produce the food we need and maintain a balance with the ecology of their land.

Farmers of the new millennium are recognizing the importance of maintaining that balance and have turned to farming methods that make their farms "environmentally friendly."

Thousands of acres of rice fields in the Heartland are flooded enticing millions of ducks, geese and other water fowl to use the areas as safe habitats as they make their way along the Pacific Flyway.

By flooding the fields following harvest farmers can supply needed habitat for wildlife. While it feeds the waterfowl, the birds help to weed the fields, decompose the rice straw and add nutrients to the soil.

SAY IT WITH WINE

And they said...
"Wine is the most civilized thing in the world."
—Ernest Hemingway

"I cook with wine, sometimes I even add it to the food."
—Anonymous

"Good wine is a necessity of life for me."
—Thomas Jefferson

"God made only water, but man made wine."
—Victor Hugo

"It's a naive domestic Burgundy without any breeding, but I think you'll be amused by its presumption."
—James Thurber

"I made wine out of raisins so I wouldn't have to wait for it to age."
—Steven Wright

"What contemptible scoundrel stole the cork from my lunch?"
—W.C. Fields

PASTA WITH TOMATOES, MOZZARELLA AND BASIL

SERVES 4–6
Submitted by Evelyn Miliate, Head Chef, BelAir Market in Gold River, CA

2 lbs - fresh tomatoes, diced small
1 - bunch fresh basil leaves, julienned
1 - large clove garlic, minced (or pressed)
4 oz - fresh mozzarella cheese or soft teleme, cut into 1/4" pieces
1/2 - teaspoon red pepper flakes
1/4 - cup extra virgin olive oil
salt and pepper to taste
1 lb - penne pasta
1 - cup fresh Parmesan cheese, grated

1 Place all ingredients except pasta and Parmesan cheese in a large bowl. Cover and let sit at room temperature for 2 hours. Bring a large pot of water to boil. Add pasta. A bit of olive oil in the water will keep the pot from boiling over. Salt water lightly if you choose. Cook, uncovered until pasta is just tender (al dente). Drain and immediately mix with fresh sauce. Serve at once, topped with grated Parmesan cheese. ✣

Goes great with Italian Garlic Bread. See recipe on page 36.

PEACH QUENCHER

SERVES 1

Submitted by Marcy Masumoto - Del Rey, California peach grower

2 - cups pureed peaches (Sun Crest* variety if you can find them)
6 oz - pineapple juice
1/2 - cup frozen lemonade, concentrate
3 - cups club soda

1 Thoroughly wash, slice and remove the pits of fresh peaches. Puree peaches in blender or food processor to make 2 cups. Add pineapple juice, lemonade concentrate and club soda. Continue to blend as you add six ice cubes. Blend only until ice becomes slushy. Pour into a tall glass and garnish with a sprig of fresh mint leaves and a Sun Crest peach slice. In the off season, you may use a package of frozen peaches. ✣

**Since it is rare to find the Sun Crest peach at your local supermarket, ask for the O'Henry or any other sweet, non-cling peach.*

TO YOUR HEALTH

California's Wine Institute has been looking at the health benefits of wine and finds some interesting data in their research. Apparently there's some "good stuff" in wine that acts specifically to enhance our well being.

Studies have shown that heart disease reduction and other health-related findings apply to all beverages containing alcohol. But, several studies have found that drinkers of wine have some clear health advantages over moderate alcohol drinkers and even over non-drinkers.

The "good stuff" specifically are the antioxidants in wine. Studies have found links with the antioxidants and the prevention of heart disease and cancer.

So, drink up...moderately please.

SALMON CREAM CHEESE DIP

Submitted by Michele Lites, Registered Dietitian

12 oz - fat free cream cheese softened
8 oz - smoked salmon
1 - Tablespoon lemon juice
1/4 - cup fresh dill, finely chopped
1/4 - cup onion, chopped
4 - celery ribs
12 - red potatoes (small)
pepper to taste

1 Let cream cheese come to room temperature. Blend cream cheese, salmon, lemon juice, dill and onions in a large food processor. Place mixture into a pastry bag and refrigerate for at least 2 hours (or over night).

2 Boil potatoes and let them cool, then cut them in half and scoop out center with a melon baller. Cut celery into 4" pieces. Pipe salmon mixture onto the celery and potatoes. Arrange on a serving platter. Garnish with salmon, capers and dill. Keep chilled until the guests arrive. ✣

WHY FARM

"...I miss the money,
but not the rat race."
—Art Summerfield
Berry Farmer

There are all kinds of reasons for becoming a farmer. Some take over from aging parents. Others spend their lives training for it. Then there are those who do it as an escape.

Art Summerfield spent 5 years as an engineer; another 20 as a printer. Today he is a farmer in the foothills of the Sierra.

Art grows berries and opens up the farm for "You Pick" excursions. He makes jam because when he was a boy his mother taught him how.

If you're ever near the foothills community of Camino, look up Summerfield Berry Farms. Art will show you his jam and perhaps give you some tips on how to escape the rat race.

ROSEMARY FETA DIP

Submitted by Christopher Ranch - Gilroy

1 - cup plain yogurt
2 - sprigs of fresh rosemary (leaves only), chopped
1 - cup feta cheese, crumbled
4 - garlic cloves, finely chopped or pressed

1 Place all of the ingredients in a blender or food processor and blend until smooth. If the mixture is too thick, add a tiny bit of milk to blend. Be careful with the milk so the dip doesn't become too liquid. Place in a small dip serving dish and garnish with a light sprinkle of additional chopped rosemary leaves or a sprig of rosemary. Use as a dip for your fresh vegetable tray. Refrigerate until you are ready to serve with chips, small crackers and sliced raw vegetables. ✣

BLOSSOM SHAPED SEAFOOD DIP

Submitted by Richard Collins of California Vegetable Specialties

1/2 - small onion, minced
1/2 - cup celery, chopped
1 1/2 - cups crab, shrimp or lobster, cooked
8 oz - cream cheese, softened
1 - Tablespoon horseradish
2 - Tablespoons mayonnaise
6 - endive leaves

1 In a food processor, blend together all ingredients except the endive leaves. Do not over process. Remove the mixture from the blender and form it into a ball. Place the seafood ball on a fancy service plate. Poke the endive leaves into the dip, starting at the bottom and working your way around to the top to create a blossom effect. Encourage your guests to use the endive leaves to scoop the dip. ✣

SOUTHERN SWEET POTATOES

SERVES 10

Submitted by Michele Lites, Registered Dietitian

1 - 29 oz can sweet potatoes, drained
2/3 - cup dark brown sugar, firmly packed
2 - Tablespoons all-purpose flour
1/2 - teaspoon ground cinnamon
1/3 - cup margarine, melted
1/3 - cup pineapple juice
1 - teaspoon vanilla extract
1/3 - cup dried cranberries
1/3 - cup pineapple, crushed
baby marshmallows optional

1 Preheat oven to 350 degrees. Place drained sweet potatoes in a large, flat casserole dish. In a small mixing bowl, add and mix sugar, flour, cinnamon, melted margarine, and pineapple in order listed. Pour this mixture evenly over the sweet potatoes. If you like, top with tiny marshmallows. Bake uncovered for 20 to 30 minutes or until marshmallows brown slightly and the liquid around the sweet potatoes begins to bubble. ✣

SPICY BAKED ONIONS

SERVES 4
Submitted by Corita Gravitt, California Heartland Executive Producer

2 - large onions (red or yellow)

MARINADE:
1/2 - cup balsamic vinegar
2 - Tablespoons dark brown sugar
1 - pinch of freshly grated nutmeg*
1 - pinch of powdered cloves*

1 Preheat oven to 350 degrees.

2 Peel and slice onions into 1/4" slices. (Best seasonal onions are Walla Wallas or Maui). Grease a cookie sheet with a bit of olive oil. Place onion slices side-by-side until the pan is filled. Place onions in the 350 degree oven for about 20 minutes. Check periodically to be sure they don't get too brown. While onions are cooking, mix the marinade.

MARINADE:
3 Whisk all above ingredients together and at the perfect moment, remove the onions from the oven. Pour the vinegar mixture over the onion slices. Sprinkle with a touch of powdered cloves. Return the onions to the oven for an additional 10 minutes to finish.

SECRET INGREDIENTS = Powdered cloves and nutmeg

WATERMELON WISDOM

So you think you'd like to grow watermelons. First, a lesson in a valuable harvesting technique we'll call the "Watermelon Twist", or "pitching" the melon.

According to Mr. Nate Wright, who has been doing the "twist" for 30-years, "Pitching watermelons is like doing the twist. You get the twising rhythm going and never hold the melon or let the weight of the watermelon hit you. You've just got to pass it on."

Believe it or not, but according to Mr. Wright, during harvest time from July to September he and his co-workers pitch about 300 tons, or 30,000 watermelons a day.

How do you know when a watermelon is ripe? According to those who grow them, you're looking for a medium or high-pitched vibration when you thump it. If it thuds then it's overripe. If it pings, you've got a good one.

SPINACH LASAGNA

SERVES 8

Submitted by Carol Laffranchi, Loleta Cheese Factory - "It's the cheese!"

12 - Lasagna noodles
3 - bunches fresh spinach
2 - Tablespoons Parmesan cheese, grated
1 - cup Baker's cheese*
1 - egg white
1 - Tablespoon onion, minced
2 - Tablespoons Parsley Patch All Purpose Salt-Free Seasoning
2 - cups Loleta Creamy Jack cheese
1 - 32 oz jar Ragu Spaghetti Sauce (add extra garlic and pepper)

1 Preheat oven to 350 degrees.

2 Cook and drain the lasagna noodles according to the directions on the package. It is better if you slightly undercook the pasta. They are less likely to break apart. When they are done, run cold water over the pasta to stop the cooking process. Chop and steam the spinach until it is limp. Drain well (squeeze dry or use salad spinner). Chop further so it won't be stringy. Add Baker's Cheese, Loleta Creamy Jack cheese, onion and seasoning to the spinach then add the 1 egg white to make mixture stick together. Spray a 13" x 9" baking dish with vegetable spray. Coat bottom of the dish with enough spaghetti sauce to prevent sticking.

3 Layer the bottom of the baking dish with noodles and spread evenly with 1/3 of the spinach mixture and sauce. Top with a light coating of tomato sauce. Repeat layers, ending with sauce. Sprinkle Parmesan cheese over lasagna and bake in a 350 degree oven for 30 minutes or until bubbly. Check at 20 minutes and if it is becoming too brown, cover with aluminum foil for the final 10 minutes. Reheats well in the microwave. Let stand for 10 minutes before serving. ✣

* jack cheese can be substituted here

AGRO ART

There is aspect of farm produce that most farmers probably don't give much attention to. These days it also serves as objects of art. Professional artists and regular folks too have come to appreciate the artful aspects of fruits and vegetables.

In the little town of Penryn the popularity of "agro art" took root at that community's annual Mandarin Orange Festival. It's remarkable what can be done with a combination of fruits and vegetables. Eggplant, bell peppers, olives, chard and mustard all found interesting uses.

As art it is different. But as the people of Penryn discovered, it is also a strong enticement for bringing a community together to celebrate the work of the harvest.

SPINACH MANICOTTI

SERVES 6

Submitted by Michele Lites, Registered Dietitian

3 - cups low fat ricotta cheese
1 - cup mozzarella cheese, shredded
2 - egg whites, beaten
2 - Tablespoons fresh Italian parsley, chopped
6 - cloves garlic, finely chopped or pressed
1 - teaspoon freshly grated nutmeg*
salt and pepper to taste
10 oz - spinach (fresh or frozen, drained)
1 - 8 oz package large manicotti shells
2 - cups spaghetti sauce (Ragu with extra garlic and pepper)
1/4 - cup Parmesan cheese, grated

1 Cook manicotti according to the directions on the package. If you under cook the pasta, the shells will fill more easily. Place pasta in cold water to stop the cooking process.

2 Saute fresh finely chopped spinach and garlic in a skillet until tender.

3 In a mixing bowl, combine ricotta and mozzarella cheese, egg whites, parsley, seasonings and spinach mixture. Pour 1 cup of spaghetti sauce on the bottom of a 13" x 9" casserole dish so pasta will not stick. Fill manicotti shells with cheese mixture and place them in the casserole dish side by side. Shells can be filled easily if you put mixture in a pastry bag with a large round tip. Squeeze the right amount of mixture into each shell so they fill completely from end to end. This amount of mixture will fill 14 manicotti shells. Pour the remaining spaghetti sauce on top and add Parmesan cheese.

4 Bake covered with aluminum foil for 20 minutes at 375 degrees. Uncover and bake at 500 degrees for an additional 10 minutes. Check often to be sure the top does not get too brown. ✣

Serve with the Mediterranean Vegetable Salad (see recipe on page 62) and plenty of Italian Garlic Bread (see recipe on page 36.)

*SECRET INGREDIENT = nutmeg

GRATER

The small grater can be used as a citrus zester to remove only the colored portion of a citrus rind. When a recipe calls for a teaspoon of lemon zest, this is the tool to use.

It is also perfect for grating hard cheeses like Parmesan.

FARMER JEFFERSON

"Cultivators of the earth are the most valuable citizens. They are the most vigorous, the most independent, the most virtuous, and they are tied to their country and wedded to its liberty and interests by the most lasting bands."
—Thomas Jefferson

Thomas Jefferson understood farmers and farming. His home at Monticello was not only his house but a farm and a plantation. Four farms made up the plantation, which covered five-thousand acres. It was a center of agriculture and industry.

The heart of Jefferson's complex was Mulberry Row. Bordered by mulberry trees, it was Jefferson's plan to make it the hub of agricultural and industrial services for his Monticello home and the surrounding farms.

STUFFED BELL PEPPERS

SERVES 4–6
Submitted by Christopher Ranch - Gilroy

1 - 1 lb package ground turkey
1 - large white or yellow onion, chopped fine
3 - cloves garlic, chopped fine (or pressed)
5 - large mushrooms, chopped fine
1 1/2 - cups brown rice, cooked
1/2 - cup Monterey jack cheese
1/2 - cup mild garlic salsa
6 - green bell peppers

1 Core peppers and boil for 10 minutes. Remove from water. Run cold water over the peppers to stop the cooking process. Set aside in a shallow baking dish. While peppers are boiling, brown turkey, onion and garlic. Drain fat. Add mushrooms and saute. Add cooked rice, shredded cheese and salsa. Warm all ingredients just until the cheese is melted. Stuff the cooked ingredients into the bell peppers until they are overflowing. Heat in a 350 degree oven for 10 minutes or until stuffing is steaming hot. ✣

TOMATO - HERB CHEESE BALL

Mediterranean sun dried tomatoes from Lester Farms - Winters

8 oz - sun-dried tomatoes (in a package)
1/2 - Tablespoon fresh basil, chopped
1/2 - Tablespoon fresh oregano, chopped
1 - teaspoon fresh rosemary, chopped
1 - green onion, finely chopped
4 - cloves garlic, finely chopped (or pressed)
2 - 8 oz packages of fat free cream cheese
2/3 - cup pine nuts*

1 Soak the sun-dried tomatoes in water for five minutes and then drain. Place tomatoes in blender or food processor and chop into small pieces (do not puree). Set aside. Next, chop by hand the basil, oregano, rosemary, green onion and garlic.

2 Mix all of the above ingredients with two packages of softened cream cheese. Stir until all ingredients are combined. Form the mixture into two equal sized balls and wrap them in plastic wrap. Chill for an hour. Remove balls from plastic wrap. Coat each ball with lightly toasted pine nuts and place on a serving plate surrounded with a variety of crackers. ✣

*SECRET INGREDIENT = pine nuts

LOCKE

It's hard to establish when a busy, rural farming community becomes an historic treasure, but the tiny Chinese delta community of Locke certainly fits the profile.

Founded in 1915, Locke was populated by Chinese merchants and farm workers who were forced to leave their fire ravaged community in nearby Walnut Grove.

Three to four thousand Chinese came into the area to construct levees. Once the levees were built or repaired, and the land was adequate for agricultural use, many Chinese stayed in the delta to become farm workers and successful tenant farmers.

At the height of development fifteen-hundred people occupied Locke with about 600 permanent residents. Today 80 to 90 people live there, sharing their stories with the scores of tourists who visit this jewel of heartland history.

GRADE AA FRESH

If you're average and live in the United States, you reportedly eat 255 eggs a year. We weren't always that keen about eating eggs, but things have apparently changed.

About 26-million hens work hard every day, producing eggs on the heartland's egg ranches. Chicken eggs are what we eat most of the time and they come primarily from the Single Comb White Leghorn.

Eggs, of course, come in many sizes and colors. Quail eggs are a dainty, speckled novelty that make up less than one-percent of our egg consumption. Ostrich eggs are so strong you can stand on them. One ostrich egg equals 30 hen eggs; great for large omelettes.

TURKEY MEATBALLS

SERVES 4
Submitted by Michele Lites, Registered Dietitian

1 lb - ground turkey
1/4 - cup onion, chopped
1/4 - cup green bell pepper, chopped
1 - egg white
3 - cloves garlic, finely chopped (or pressed)
salt and pepper to taste
1 - 26 oz jar of chunky spaghetti sauce
1 1/2 - cups BBQ sauce

1 Preheat oven to 400 degrees. Pour spaghetti sauce and barbecue sauce into a crock-pot or chafing dish and simmer on low to warm the sauce.

2 Place the remaining ingredients in a large bowl and mix well. Roll mixture into 1 oz balls using your hands, spoon or melon baller. Makes about 24 meatballs. Place meatballs into a baking pan and bake in the oven for 12 minutes. Add meatballs to the sauce. Use toothpicks for serving. ✣

NEW WORLD FOODS

According to the Old Farmer's Almanac, the so called "New World" cuisine is catching on. For the uninitiated, the new fare features ingredients such as coconuts, yucca, shrimp, mangoes, citrus fruits, almonds, kumquats and coffee.

The Almanac says "New World" cuisine focuses any exotic/tropical blend of tastes. That can include Vietnamese soft spring rolls with paw-paw slaw and peanut dipping sauce.

From border to border, California is a major supplier of the foods that make the "new world" so popular. Pomegranates and pecans, avocados and almonds, tangerines and figs and a fruit crate full of other products are grown in the heartland. Welcome to the New World!

CALIFORNIA TOMATO MARINADE

Submitted by Carole Gostanian of Grandpa Charlie's Marinades

1 - Tablespoon red wine vinegar
1 - green bell pepper
1 - red bell pepper
1 - large onion (white or yellow)
1 - cup tomatoes (freshly chopped)
1/2 - cup chopped fresh parsley
3 - cloves garlic, minced
1 - lemon (juice only)
salt and pepper to taste

1 Finely chop the above vegetables. Add the red wine vinegar, lemon juice, salt and pepper to taste. You can make quick work of this by tossing it all into your food processor or blender. You can do a version of this marinade by adding dry red wine instead of the vinegar. Marinate meat, poultry, fish or vegetables for at least 30 minutes or overnight. Use also to baste barbecue meats. ✣

TOMATO HERBED RICOTTA SALAD

SERVES 4
Submitted by Joanne Weir of Weir Cooking

1/2 lb - ricotta or feta cheese
2 - Tablespoons fresh basil leaves, chopped
1 - Tablespoon fresh mint leaves, chopped
1 - Tablespoon fresh chives, chopped
1 - teaspoon fresh oregano leaves, chopped
1 - teaspoon fresh thyme leaves, chopped
5 - large ripe tomatoes, 1/4" slices
1/2 lb - colored cherry tomatoes, red, orange, yellow mix, halved
4 - Tablespoons extra virgin olive oil
3 - Tablespoons balsamic vinegar
coarsely ground salt and black pepper
fresh basil, mint, oregano and thyme leaves for garnish

1 Crumble the ricotta or feta cheese in a bowl. Add the basil, mint, chives, oregano and thyme and mix together until all herbs are on the outside of the cheese. Set aside.

2 Place the tomatoe slices on a serving platter, overlapping slightly. Scatter the cherry tomatoes on top. Season with salt and pepper.

3 In a small bowl, whisk together the olive oil and vinegar. Scatter the cheese over the tomatoes and pour on the dressing. Scatter herb sprigs for garnish. Serve chilled. ✣

SANTE THAI VEGGIE SALAD

Submitted by Beverly Berkley of David Berkley's Fine Wines & Specialty Foods

2 - red bell peppers, thinly julienned
2 - yellow bell peppers, thinly julienned
1 - head broccoli, flowers only, cut in quarters
2 - large carrots, sliced at an angle (1/2")
1 1/2 lbs - fresh snap peas, sliced
3/4 lb - fresh Shiitake mushrooms, sliced
1 - 15 oz can baby corn, drained well, sliced
1 - 5 oz can sliced water chestnuts, drained well
1/4 lb - fresh bean sprouts
1/2 - bunch green onion, thinly sliced
1/2 - head Napa cabbage, very thinly sliced

DRESSING:
3 oz - fresh ginger
3 - cloves fresh garlic, finely chopped
1/4 - cup mango chutney
1/4 - cup sesame oil
1 1/2 - cup granulated sugar
2 - Tablespoons crushed red chilies
1/4 - cup soy sauce
1 1/2 - cup rice wine vinegar
1/4 - cup water

1 Puree the ginger and garlic in a food processor. Thoroughly combine ginger and garlic mixture with remaining dressing ingredients and chill before serving.

2 Combine all veggies. Pour over dressing and toss to coat. Allow to sit for 1/2 hour or more so the flavors will meld. Serve chilled. ✣

INDEX

F

G

H

I

K

L

M

N

O

P

R

S

T

V

W

Z